Books by Matthew Lowes

Spirituality

That Which is Before You (2020)
When You are Silent It Speaks (2021)
A Billion Fingers Point at the Moon (2022)
Lighting the Sacred Fire (coming in 2023)

Fiction

The End of All Things (2018)

Games

Elements of Chess (2012)
Dungeon Solitaire: Labyrinth of Souls (2016)
Dungeon Solitaire: Devil's Playground (2018)

A BILLION FINGERS POINT AT THE MOON

A BILLION FINGERS POINT AT THE MOON

MATTHEW LOWES

DECIPHERING SPIRITUAL LANGUAGE

Empty Press

2022

A Billion Fingers Point at the Moon:
Deciphering Spiritual Language
/ Matthew Lowes
ISBN
978-1-952073-04-5 (pbk.)

Typeset in
Minion Pro by Robert Slimbach
Source Sans pro by Paul D. Hunt

Empty Press

matthewlowes.com

TABLE OF CONTENTS

Your word is a light for my path.
—Psalms 119:105

But of what use are names when reality is so near?
—Sri Nisargadatta Maharaj

FORWARD

When I was nine, I tried to read *The Iliad*. It didn't go very well, and that failed effort discouraged me from reading anything more challenging than *The Savage Sword of Conan* comics for some time. In retrospect, though, my youthful ambition was probably a sign rather than an impediment. For around the age of seventeen, I fell in love with books. As a literature major at university, I developed an interest in literary theory and philosophy of language. Eventually, I even married a linguist, pursued a writing career, and taught high school English. I wrote a lot of fantasy, horror, and science fiction, but in the back of my mind I always thought I would eventually write some kind of book about language. I knew it would touch upon some of what is strange about words, metaphor, and meaning, but I never thought it would really be a book about spirituality. Nevertheless … here we are. So may these words guide readers *beyond* all words, and toward illumination, true happiness, and an end to suffering.

Acknowledgements

Many thanks to my teachers, students, friends, family, and loved ones. Thanks to all those who read and commented on early drafts of this book. And thanks to all those who read the books that preceded this one. I am ever-grateful, and your contributions to this work are deeply appreciated.

A BILLION FINGERS POINT AT THE MOON

INTRODUCTION

"Don't mistake a finger for the moon" is an old Zen saying. It reminds us that spiritual teachings only point toward the truth; they are not the truth itself. There is an actual moon out there, and any finger pointing toward it only indicates which direction to look. If you know this *completely* already, through and through, and how it pertains to *everything,* you can stop reading now. In that case, you would already be gazing at the moon, enraptured by its wonder and glory. If not, I encourage you to read on.

This is the third book in a series about spirituality and enlightenment. The first book contains an account of my awakening, insights and teachings, as well as a brief overview of spiritual practices. The second book contains a more detailed discussion of the spiritual journey as a whole. The aim of this book is to address the language of spirituality and attempt to clear up some of the confusion surrounding its vocabulary. As such, it is an elaboration on what I have already said, a final attempt to push readers toward clarity, before going deeper into the subject of spiritual practice.

In some ways, this is a challenging topic, insofar as it directly touches upon the ambiguities and difficulties of language itself. But that shouldn't discourage anyone. In some ways, our endeavor here is quite simple. The core of our discussion will be a straight-forward examination of the meanings of various words used to describe spiritual concepts and how the words themselves add to the confusion seekers and practitioners so often encounter. In this process, we will get ourselves into tangles and out of tangles, all in an effort to see through the biggest tangle of all — the mind itself.

No doubt, there will be times when the reader will feel confused. That is to be expected. This is tricky stuff, and we will be *deliberately* throwing ourselves into the tangles. My suggestion to confused readers is this: Keep reading, but don't struggle too much with the material. If necessary, treat the text as a kind of strange enigmatic poem — for understanding can begin far below our conscious perception. Remember, I am not trying to tell you how things are or explain the universe. Nor do I pretend to be an expert on philosophy or religions. This is not an ordinary book, which would present an argument to intellectually grasp and accept or reject. This text is a kind of spell to dispel the magic of delusion. Do your part by reading and trying to understand ... but also allow it to do its part by letting it wash over and through you, unhindered by grasping or resistance.

The words with which we describe the world of spirituality are diverse and enticing. They include the exotic names of many gods and supernatural beings, mind-boggling concepts of cosmic proportion, esoteric practices, extraordinary states, other worlds, and ultimate goals, ends, and truths. This vocabulary has accumulated from a wide range of teachers, traditions, lineages, movements, philosophies, and religions. On the surface, when taken as a whole, it does not represent a cohesive system of thought. Even if one begins to dig into it, the overwhelming feeling may be one of endless contradiction, conflict, and confusion.

If we kept digging, however, until we got to the bottomless bottom of it all, everything would become clear. Then we would see that so much confusion is caused not only by the diversity of languages and the course of history and ideas, and by a multitude of poor translations and misinterpretations, but also by something more fundamental to language and thought itself. The confusion starts with the inherent ambiguity of words and the dualistic traps of systems and concepts. And beyond all that, we would behold a shining unassailable truth which the vast panoply of words but dimly attempt to convey.

The heart of these discussions is rooted in direct, immediate recognition and limitless awareness. However, we will have to utilize words and ideas from various spiritual traditions, and all the ambiguities of language will be in play. In this sense, I'll be drawing on a broad but limited kind of knowledge. Although I've read a number of books, I am not an expert in philosophy, science, or religious doctrine — nor do I have any desire to rival scholars in addressing the details of those topics. So it's important to remember that we'll be attempting here to peer *through* various systems of thought. Don't get distracted by philosophical, scientific, doctrinal, or dogmatic disputes. That would be missing the entire point.

Words themselves are an incredibly fascinating topic, both from a historical and philosophical perspective. With regard to spirituality, or any other subject, language is the medium of every assertion, criticism, or discussion. For this reason, that is where we'll begin. But don't make the mistake of thinking this is a book about words or language. This is a book about the moon. The book itself is only another finger, pointing at that which is beyond all words.

1

SPIRITUALITY CONFUSED

Those who went before me
Had left their mark —
Their breadcrumbs were scattered
Across creation.
And yet I wandered,
Looking for the way.

THE MAZE OF CONFUSION

Spirituality itself can be a maze of confusion. Anybody who has cultivated a sincere interest in understanding the nature of reality — who they are and what is really happening — will be confronted with a mind-boggling array of questions, ideas, theories, philosophies, theologies, cosmologies, advice, methods, and practices. Whatever our background, we typically view this vast terrain of words as a landscape of things to accept or reject, to believe or disbelieve, to ignore or implement.

As we go about making judgments about all these things, already we have entered an infinite labyrinth, which exists within and yet always veils the truth we seek. How long will we wander in its halls? To what depths and into what darkness will we venture? How many doors will we open? How many battles will we fight? What treasure will we cling to? What doom will we dread? And is there any way out?

Human beings get involved in spirituality and its branches through various means. Initially, we are indoctrinated into an inherited system of thought: a religion, belief structure, or world-view. This system gives us some fundamental ideas upon which to rest our questions, our fears, our longings, and all our thoughts about who we are, where we are, and how things work. From there, we may delve deeper into the system we have and/or encounter and adopt other thought systems.

From these systems we learn the name of God or that there is no god, or that there are many gods. We learn of consciousness, spirits, or souls. We learn of angels and demons, sinners and saints, heavens and hells. We learn of saviors, buddhas, and jivanmuktas. We learn of human beings, plants, and animals. We learn of worlds and universes. We learn of cause and effect, past and future, space and time, birth and death, delusion and enlightenment.

At some point, we may hear "the good news" or it may really sink in that there *is* a truth that can set us free, that enlightenment is real, that salvation is more than just an idea. The sacred fire is lit, and we set off on our quest for the ultimate truth. But whatever system we learn and believe, whatever combination of ideas we have, whatever concepts we adopt, whatever words we use, the truth lies forever beyond. However far we go in our search, the truth always lies *beyond* beyond. And so we never *really* feel satisfied with any system of thought alone.

Many people have the experience of cycling through doubts and beliefs, searching and settling, or denouncing and adopting. For example, we may come to doubt the ideas we have about our inherited belief system when it doesn't sufficiently answer or address our innermost feelings, or when it's challenged by other convincing observations and enticing ideas. We may search for deeper answers within a given system or alternate answers outside of the system.

Wherever we end up, however, we soon find ourselves in the same situation. Perhaps we have a different vocabulary, a more complex or more simple picture, but fundamentally we are no better off, no closer to the truth. We are still lost in the maze of confusion, entranced by words and ideas, thoughts and concepts.

Wander around for a while and it may seem hopeless. If we go far enough, however, one thing becomes clear: we will never find our way out of this confusion through a new combination of words or beliefs. Relatively speaking, some words may move us closer or farther from the truth, but ultimately the particulars are not what's important. The truth beyond words is always present. So what becomes important is seeing *through* words, seeing *through* ideas, seeing *through* beliefs and recognizing the reality in which they all appear.

LANGUAGE AND MEANING

What is the difficulty with language? At first glance, we may say there is no difficulty at all. As long as we're speaking the same language, we understand each other well enough. When things are ambiguous or vague, we just clarify and it all works out. Even in translations, it often seems that with enough clarification we can understand the words of another language just fine.

That's all well and good when you want to know where the bathroom is or how much a hamburger costs, but perhaps not as much when you want to know what reality is, what God is, or who and what you really are. Words are very useful when it comes to relative, practical matters, but have proven quite cumbersome when it comes to fundamental, existential questions.

In the same way Newtonian physics is good enough to calculate orbital trajectories but does not account for relativity or quantum mechanics, we might say language is practical but somewhat limited. This analogy might suggest that a more sophisticated language or vocabulary would solve whatever deficits a given language might have. While that may be true up to a point, the difficulty goes much deeper.

Even our most up-to-date theories about the universe cannot fundamentally tell us what reality is, because reality itself does not stand in relation to anything else. One cannot get outside of it, so no distinctions can make sense of it. Similarly, language cannot encompass anything that lies outside of itself. The word *ineffable* can be spoken, but what is actually ineffable cannot be. It is beyond the scope of language, and it's telling that we have a word to express that.

This is all to say, there is a fundamental limitation to words — language, ideas, concepts, explanations, and so on — that separates the conceptual from the actual. A *tree* is only an idea, a concept, delineated through thought and language. The actuality is always without limits, and beyond all words. In this way, words, thoughts, and concepts are the garments of *maya,* the illusion which separates us from our true nature. When the subject of our discourse is the ineffable reality beyond the veil of illusion, how are we to proceed?

So here, right at the beginning of our discussion on the language of spirituality, we are already running into this difficulty.

This is difficult stuff to process when we are still so early in our discussion, but we have to get this on the table at the outset. There is a rich tradition of philosophy of language that delves into how language conveys meaning and so on. I have no desire to get into the various arguments. But suffice it to say, there is great mystery in language and a kind magic to words, which great minds struggle to understand.

That language is so commonplace belies its great mystery. Whether we are talking about a tree or God, the mundane world or the supreme reality, delusion or enlightenment, the nature of language — it's difficulties, ambiguities, and limitations — must be folded into the discussion. So we will proceed in subsequent chapters through a collection of seemingly conflicting or contradicting ideas in an attempt to make clear where the language of spirituality stops … and the reality begins.

History and Culture

The origin of human language is a contested subject among linguists and anthropologists. They might place the first language anywhere between millions of years ago to just a hundred thousand years ago, depending on whether it sprang up more or less complete when the necessary components appeared or came about gradually over a long period of time. For our purposes, the how and when are not as important as the interaction between history, culture, and various languages.

Whenever human language appeared, its forms would have been inextricably linked to culture — then, as it is now. Even if in the beginning there was only one language or proto-language used by one group of people, over time, through interaction, migration, and innovation, there would soon be many languages used by many groups of people, just as there are today. In times past, the diversity of languages would have been immense, with many unique languages spoken by just small groups of people.

Languages themselves change. Old English, for example, is incomprehensible to speakers of modern English, and every language we know today has antecedents. These changes are a big topic — new vocabulary is adopted, sounds shift, usage evolves, and so on. It's happening all the time. Some languages are dying out, current languages are changing, and new languages are appearing. It only seems relatively static from our day-to-day point of view. But it is more like a roiling ocean of sound and meaning, with currents and eddies constantly morphing into new shapes and patterns.

Each language — as it comes into being, changes, and disappears — shapes and is shaped by the cultures in which it is used. This vast ongoing history is not only the history of our words and languages, but also a history of our ideas, our stories, and our discourse. While words are always associated with concepts, they are not fixed to them, and the concepts themselves are not fixed either. It is not difficult to find words that meant one thing at one time and something totally different in another time, or even within the same time but in a different context. Nor is it difficult to find concepts associated with multiple words from different cultures or even from the same culture.

With all this in mind, it is easy to imagine the difficulties in interpreting language used to describe and explain spiritual matters — especially when considering ancient texts and cross-cultural translations. Can a modern person truly understand what is said in the Vedas, or by the Desert Fathers, or by the Six Patriarchs?

Inevitably, the answer is no … and also yes! As frustrating as that may be, that's exactly the kind of situation we're going to be dealing with here.

On the one hand, we cannot directly know and experience the cultural and day-to-day context of such language. In other words, we cannot really know the thoughts behind the words. We can only know our own thoughts. This is true even when interpreting the words of modern teachers speaking our own language. On the other hand, while words may only refer to thoughts, they *point* toward a direct experience which is beyond thoughts or words.

With regard to spirituality, it is especially true that the intended purpose of the words is not only to recreate thoughts, but to point toward that which lies beyond them. And if we recognize that direct experience, then all words — regardless of language or culture or time — become clear and transparent.

Religion and Philosophy

Again, there are a number of things we need to get on the table before we take up the task of deciphering words. In addition to the overarching difficulties of language and meaning in general, and the difficulties presented by history and culture, time and translation, we must add the specific influence of religion and philosophy.

Perhaps the simplest way to account for the influence of religion and philosophy on language is to say that they have acted like cultures within cultures. Each system of thought tends to adopt a specific set of terms. Sometimes these terms are borrowed or adapted from antecedent or parallel systems, and sometimes they are a reaction against them. They include theological, ontological, and scientific concepts, as well as the names of gods, other beings, and phenomena.

Each religion or philosophy is distinct insofar as it distinguishes itself from others through differences in terminology, concepts, stories, dogma, doctrines, beliefs, and practices. Certainly there are vast, kaleidoscopic differences on this level — which is the level of language and conceptual experience. Presumably, however, all these systems of thought are, at their heart, good faith attempts to articulate the same fundamental reality. That is, the kaleidoscope of multicolored forms are all illuminated by the same light. One form may be square and another triangular, one red and one blue, but the light that shines is the same light for all.

It would be silly to say there not differences between systems of thought. Of course there are. But the differences are differences in systems of thought, not in reality, which has no thoughts attached to it. Within this reality, thoughts come and go — good ones and bad ones, right ones and wrong ones, similar ones and strange ones. In a billion different languages they are expressed and argued over, adopted and adapted, rejected and discarded. While all this goes on, reality itself is ever-present. It never varies, never falters, never changes. It cannot be *right* because it is not an idea and there is no alternative. It cannot be *wrong* because it is self-evident.

Reality itself cannot be touched or described because nothing is apart from it. So while we can acknowledge variance in religions and philosophies, to honor their deepest message we must look beyond all differences and distinctions. We must go beyond words to realize that to which they point.

One day I was browsing in the bookstore and came across a book called *God is Not One* by Stephen Prothero. Curious, I glanced at the back. The book seemed focused on the differences between religions. Nothing wrong with that, but the very examples given on the back cover spoke to the one God beyond all words, thoughts, and distinctions. For a few major religions, the text posed a problem and an offered solution. For Islam, the problem is pride and the solution is submission. For Christianity, the problem is sin and the solution is salvation. For Buddhism, the problem is suffering and the solution is awakening. For Judaism, the problem is exile and the solution is a return to God.

Stephen Prothero is a well-respected scholar, and I would not presume to question his knowledge or command of his subject. I have deep respect for scholarly work, but the point of such work is to make distinctions, express ideas, and form arguments. That is not our purpose here. In any case, my comments are more about the cover copy than the substance of his book. Pride, sin, suffering, and exile may all be very distinct problems on the level of ideas for the purposes of an argument. But if we take these ideas as an array of pointing fingers and orient ourselves in the direction they point, then pride is nothing other than sin, sin is nothing other than suffering, and suffering is nothing other than exile from God. Likewise, submission, salvation, awakening, and return all point in the same direction. All these words point toward the ever-present divine reality, without ever being apart from it.

I bring up this anecdote because it illustrates our endeavor over the course of this book. In examining the language of spirituality, we will touch on both difference and sameness, without leaving either out. In so doing, the purpose of the text is to orient the reader toward that which is beyond any system of thought. For the truth all words point to can be nothing other than the reality in which words themselves appear.

Seeing Words for What They Are

Let us be clear: if we aim to realize that which is beyond all words, thoughts, and concepts, then clearly words cannot take us all the way there. No amount of discussion, description, definition, or clarification will — on their own — allow us to arrive at the conclusion we seek. No language, ancient or modern, can come any closer to the truth than another. And no technical, scientific, philosophical, or spiritual vocabulary will ever encompass reality itself.

To go beyond, we must truly go beyond words. But that doesn't mean words are entirely useless on the path. Silence may be the greatest teaching, but not all are ready to hear it. The great treasures of oral teaching and spiritual literature are testaments to the power of words in orienting and preparing people for awakening. They do this by dispelling confusion, fear, and doubt … and then by dispelling themselves — leaving the seeker free to encounter reality unhindered by the veil of words, thoughts, and concepts.

We could say there is a two-step process: first helping to remove some obstacles that language might address, then removing the obstacle of language itself. Without the second part of the process, language itself — words, ideas, concepts, and models — becomes a trap. That is when the finger is mistaken for the moon. Don't do that. Keep going until the finger disappears and the radiant moon encompasses everything.

In some traditions, a practitioner is given a mantra or a prayer to repeat. The words may have some meaning to spiritually orient the person, to help set their intention on finding the truth, on letting go of the ego-self, or on surrendering to the divine. At the beginning of practice, the words themselves may be a bulwark against the onslaught of ideas — of fears, desires, doubts, and other egoic demands. Through repetition and focus, all these competing thoughts become more and more quiet, leaving only the mantra at the center of attention. The light beyond may begin to shine through, but the words are still present. Finally, if we see these words for what they are, the words themselves will fall away, and nothing is left but the divine light.

Words do not really refer to anything. The words themselves are only ideas. Whether we seem to encounter them from within or without, they are never anything more than ideas. Any subject, object, or world we imagine the words refer to is a confabulation. From the very beginning, there has never been anything but the divine light, and all things are nothing but this light.

The priceless treasure of words that make up the oral teachings and spiritual literature is like a great mantra. This wondrous prayer … this unending song … is chanted by the universe itself. It calls us to join in and set out upon the path. Even without our conscious understanding, it unwinds our confusion. To take up this great mantra is not without its difficulties and not without traps and obstacles. But if we follow it to the end and see it for what it is, even this great mantra will fall away, and the divine reality will be revealed.

What Lies Beyond Words

We have already stated that the truth lies beyond all words. We have mentioned the divine light, the reality, and the limitless One. While these words point to what I'm getting at, they are still only ideas. Anything more I say will also be in the realm of ideas. Even as ideas, to many people these words will seem very abstract, vague, and unhelpful. Perhaps we can point more effectively with something a little more mundane and concrete.

I have previously used the example of a tree, and I see no reason not to use it again. It's a good example, and I like trees. When we think of a tree, an image may appear in the mind. When we look at a tree, an image also appears in the mind. What is the image? What is the tree? What is the mind?

A tree is only an idea, a concept. There are no actual trees in the world. What we see or what we imagine to be a tree has no real limits. It is so intimately connected to the universe out of which it has grown that we could say it is simply the universe itself. And we are no different. Because the mind itself is also only an idea, it cannot take in the whole universe. Having already separated itself off from the rest of the universe, the ego-self divides the rest of the universe into similar pieces it calls things … and in this case "trees" and "minds."

While we can certainly talk about trees and individual selves or minds — and these things can be said to exist as ideas or concepts — in actuality, there are no trees, there are no egos, and there are no minds … at least beyond the ideas themselves.

Furthermore, even the concept of ideas is also an idea that can only be said to exist in the impermanent, effervescent realm of ideas. It sounds like a paradox, but that too is just an idea. If we go deep enough into it, the whole thing may collapse into a reality beyond ideas. What is that reality? There really is no word for it … but we might say that all words ultimately refer to that.

Each of the aforementioned words and each of the words we will discuss going forward relating to the self, the world, cause and effect, God, spiritual practice, and enlightenment can be collapsed into an idea with a variety of distinctions and qualities to be argued over. But each can also be expanded, dropped, or made transparent, and when that happens for everything all at once, what lies beyond will be apparent.

So let's get on with it!

2

THE SELF QUESTION

There is nothing behind these eyes
And nothing commands these hands.
There is no inside to this body,
And no outside of this mind.
There is no subject in this experience,
And no object in this consciousness.
There is nowhere for anything to rest,
Except in the heart of mystery.

THE IDENTITY QUESTION

What issues do the world's spiritual traditions attempt to address? It seems that one of the core issues, if not *the* core issue, is one of identity. Who or what is a human being, and can our existence be placed in some context? Many of the other issues, such as the nature of the universe itself and the laws that govern it, as well as the nature of any God or gods, how humans should behave, and so on can be seen as arising out of this fundamental question about the nature of our own being. If, for example, there were no human beings, the question of the universe and everything else would not arise … at least for us.

So in addressing the language of spirituality, we will begin with a discussion about the nature of this identity. We will examine the terminology used by some of the world's traditions, and try to unravel some of the confusion words may inadvertently cause for someone looking to get a clear picture or to orient themselves on the spiritual path.

The identity question arises from our own experience of being a particular person, a personality with thoughts and memories, hopes and dreams, desires and fears. We have a feeling of being a separate and distinct entity, with a body and mind, moving about in an objective world full of various things. It is natural to ask, "Who am I?" That is why so much of human culture helps to give us an answer — through naming, family, tribe, ethnicity, caste, country, history, religion, beliefs, and so on.

The world's traditions have tried to pin down this personal entity, in one way or another, through a variety of terms and concepts. And so we have, in various times and cultures, thought about a person's *spirit* or *soul.* We have spoken of having a *self* or an *ego.* And we have associated this entity with a *mind* and with *consciousness.* We have envisioned ourselves as being this individual entity, encased within a body, moving through time from an imagined birth to an imagined death.

At the same time, the traditions have almost universally acknowledged that this entity-experience exists within a larger context that it may call the world, creation, or the universe. They may argue about whether the entity is *born into* or *born out of* the world, and what and where it is when it is not *here,* but most seem to agree upon this basic description of our lives.

If we are going by words alone, whatever terminology we choose or even if we choose to consider them all, we will surely be left with some confusion. Am I a soul, a mind, or an ego? And what about an ego-self? What's that all about? There are even people today who will say you are your brain or your nervous system. Everybody is looking for a word to call this thing … this self that we experience. Everybody is looking for some *thing* to identify it with, as if by identifying it and giving it a name, we could waylay our existential dread.

In the process of naming ourselves, we bring in all kinds of other words and concepts, and we completely confuse the matter. We begin to argue over why one term is better than another, or we vie for authority by denying the existence of one idea while supporting the existence of a different idea. And on and on and on … all throughout history this game has gone on.

So in this chapter we will be examining the terminology of self-hood, the various distinctions people have made, the clarification and confusion that arises from such distinctions, and where it all may be pointing.

A Tale of Two Selves

In the spiritual discourse, there seems to be a lot of debate and confusion over the idea of a *self*. Is there a self or no self? What is a self? And perhaps most interesting: Is there more than one kind of self? Could there be two selves? For example, is there a kind of lesser self and a greater self? Does everyone have an individual self or is there just one self?

We see these ideas popping up all the time in a wide range of traditions. The basic ideas take on a multitude of forms and variations. If we start to examine some terms, differences and similarities begin to take shape, depending on one's disposition.

In the Hindu tradition, there is a concept of the individual self, called the *atman,* and the supreme self or primordial self, called the *paramatman.* In some indigenous traditions, there is a sense of a spirit and the great spirit or great mystery, what the Algonquian language calls *Gitche Manitou.* In Judeo-Christian circles there is a *soul,* which is like the *atman* or *spirit,* and a *God,* which can be likened to *paramatman* or *Gitche Manitou.* Even psychologists get in on the fun with the *false self* and *true self.* And not to be outdone, the Buddhist tradition has a concept of "no self," which seems to deny the existence of a self altogether. If you go into it a bit, though, this "no self" begins to sound an awful lot like the paramatman, which is without individuality, and the self that is denied begins to sound an awful lot like a false self or an illusory self.

There you have it. With just a few broad traditions in the mix, we're already in an incredible tangle! Hopefully you can see by now — without me going into exhaustive detail — that if we went into more detail about the distinctions, philosophies, and histories of such ideas, this tangle would only get bigger and bigger. So we'll leave that to scholars. And we'll save our own discussion of terms like mind, consciousness, and reality for a little later in the chapter.

I'm not saying all these ideas perfectly line up or are exactly the same. That is not the point. The words are clearly different. They have different origins, histories, and philosophical context. Each idea relies on different concepts, images, and conceptions. Nevertheless, generally speaking, again and again we see variations on a little self and a big self, the individual and the absolute, the soul and God, the personal spirit and the great mystery, the illusory self and reality. So we might characterize this general idea as the individual self and the absolute self. Or … you know … choose whatever terms you like. On this level it is just a matter of taste, aesthetic preference, poetic license, or traditional lineage.

The little self is associated with the individual personality, the body, the ego, life and death, volition, preference, judgment, and decision making. This is what I sometimes call the ego-self. It is a sense of being something and someone, a separate and finite being living in a larger reality. With the ego-self, we have the feeling that we are a distinct entity, contained within a body, existing in a world, and moving through time between an imagined birth and an imagined death. It might be called a spirit, a soul, personal consciousness, or just a person. This little self, insofar as it can be said to be anything, is always a *thing*, defined and inscribed by words. Although we do not really understand who or what we are, nevertheless the feeling persists.

The big self is associated with concepts of oneness or union with the universe, with God, or with an ultimate reality. It is revealed when the little self becomes transparent, dissipates, dissolves into or unites with the transcendent. What exactly happens to the little self — whether it "unites with" or "is destroyed" and so on — is here just a matter of words. The utter insignificance of the little self, once this big self is realized, is why the ego-self is sometimes called the false self. The big self has many names: The Self, Brahman, God, Dharmakaya, Tao, and so on, including the names of many gods and metaphysical concepts. As words, as concepts, they are only concepts, and so always limited to a small self. They are, nevertheless, concepts which overtly point toward the great mystery, which is beyond all words, all concepts, and all thought.

That is the basic lexical landscape. Most of the confusion that arises on account of the words does not arise through an inability to understand the concepts. Some, yes, but more confusion is due to ambiguity about whether one is talking about small self or big self. And beyond that, there is also the fundamental confusion that arises due to mistaking concepts for reality in the first place.

So if we're approaching these words, we should try to be clear about what's being discussed. We should try to understand what is being affirmed or denied, what is called real or unreal, and what that means on the level of concepts. But we should also understand whether those concepts pertain to the individual or the universal. And most importantly, we should attempt to orient ourselves in the direction of what is pointed at in reality — that is, beyond words, beyond concepts, and beyond levels.

SELF AND NON-SELF

There are those who say there is nothing but the Self, while others claim there is nothing called a self whatsoever. Seemingly, the two positions could not be more diametrically opposed. Confusion abounds on this issue of self and non-self, with many staking their faith on the idea of non-self, and others making a god of the universal self. If one is not lodged in one camp or another, taking it's vocabulary as one's very own, what is one to make of all this? Which is it? And under what conditions?

Around the time Buddhism emerged in the context of what we now call Hinduism, the two views — and a variety of other views — coexisted in a similar historical, cultural, linguistic, and philosophical landscape. This question of the self and its place in the ideological landscape was a defining factor for many different movements. So it makes sense to look deeper into this question.

Let's first take a moment to acknowledge this is a simplification of doctrinal differences. The diversity of views in Hinduism and Buddhism is actually much greater than what is suggested. Being everything, nothing, or something in between, nobody really knows what the self is, so naturally there are a lot of different ideas. But all seem to agree it is a central question, or at least a significant one.

The Buddhist tradition emphasizes the impermanence of all things. Nothing is lasting, not the body, not the mind, not the senses, not any thought or image or idea, and so on. Since these are the various things we tend to identify as constituting our self, there can be no real self, at least no little self. For it is only the individual self that is denied — the soul, or the atman. Instead, what we think of as an individual is just an aggregate of thoughts, beyond which there is no distinct entity — only emptiness. But this emptiness is also the great fullness of being. Some might even call it *paramatman*.

The Hindu tradition emphasizes the unchanging fullness of reality itself. While some maintain atman is the individual person, they also say that atman is ultimately identical to paramatman — the big self — which is also the same as Brahman. So ... is there an atman or not? If not, there is no atman to deny. When the individual self is realized to be nothing other than the universal self, the former notion of the individual is revealed as a kind of illusion. And Brahman, being the ultimate reality, encompasses emptiness and fullness alike.

These two traditions are really not that different. Within the apparent contradiction of concepts, there is just the play of words and language! Again and again, all throughout history, new people confront the same issue with different words. On a grand scale, they are from completely different cultures and completely different times, using a completely different language and completely different metaphors. On a smaller scale they can be neighbors, geographically, temporally, or culturally. In this case, the Buddhist vocabulary was a kind of innovative variation on the vocabulary of coexisting traditions. Buddha, after all, was not the first buddha. Others had realized before him, and had merely described their realization with different words.

If we are philosophers, historians, or religious experts, then we could debate and argue over these kinds of things forever. And as seekers we could be trapped into thinking we must discover the right view. But that is exactly the situation I wish for you to avoid. It is, to be blunt, a pointless waste of time with regard to the spiritual journey. Instead, whether you are in a Buddhist, a Hindu, or any other tradition from Christian to Atheist, go right to the heart of matter! If you are a Christian, for example, don't waste time speculating on a particular view of Jesus or arguing over a history you can never verify. Whatever Jesus you imagine is only a fiction of the mind, for you are lost in your own ideas or the ideas of others. Instead, find the Christ who is within you, here and now. Then you will know, without a doubt, the glory of God.

If you truly seek the truth, then scrabble and claw your way toward a truth that is beyond words and beyond any kind of dispute. Resolve to find out for yourself what the self is, so that you will know at last what to let go of and what to abide in.

REAL OR UNREAL

In spiritual circles, there's a lot of talk — and a lot of confusion — about what is real and what is unreal. The substance of this debate can be applied to just about everything: God, the world, objects, and so on. But the question of what is real is perhaps at its most personal, immediate, and challenging when it pertains to the self. People have a deep and abiding interest in the themselves. So the question of what is real with regard to the self goes right to the heart of their most existential concerns.

Many are fond of saying that the self is not real, that it does not exist, that there is no such thing as the self. I will not dispute it. But this view, usually derived from the *anatman* or "no-self" doctrine of Buddhism, is still just a view. As a doctrine, it is only a concept. Nevertheless, it is a very useful teaching precisely for the way it challenges the prevalent view. The idea that there is nothing called a self is shocking to most people if they really consider it. This shock itself can momentarily disrupt a person's conditioned way of thinking, opening them to inquiry, spiritual insight, or awakening.

As a teaching, however, to say "The self is not real" should be considered an opening statement, the beginning of a dialogue or inquiry, and not the end of it. It is only a useful teaching if it leads to deeper inquiry, spiritual insight, or awakening. One should investigate to find out if it's true, and not take it at face value. Even the Buddha preached that.

There is still the question: what is "real"? For many people, the self is real by virtue of the fact that in their experience, there is something they call their self. No simple statement will convince them it is not real. But the spiritual discourse is usually using the term "real" in a very specific way, not to mean *what is apparent,* but to mean what is substantively lasting, that which does not appear and disappear. It is in this sense that the self is not real, for anything that might be identified as the self turns out to be transient, insubstantial, and impermanent. When searching for the self, one will never find any *thing* which is real in this sense.

Still, this teaching may not always hit the mark. To some who are not inclined to inquire into it, the teaching of no-self may seem to deny the reality of their experience. It is actually asking you to examine the reality of your experience, but that is not always clear and some will dismiss it. So sometimes I will say, "Of course the self is real. The question is: what is it?" This is a more open-ended teaching that acknowledges the apparent reality of the self, while still spurring one on to inquiry.

I'm not kidding around with this, either. There is a Self and a No-Self which is beyond self and no-self, and it is none other than the Reality which is beyond real and unreal. Neither "The self is *not* real" nor the "The self *is* real" will get you there. But if you search for the self unrelentingly you will not find it until you find It. Then all this nonsense will be perfectly clear.

Soul and Self

In the West, most people are familiar with the idea of a soul. Whether or not they believe a person has a soul and what they think it is are up for debate, but the idea is one that speaks to the essence of a human being. In this sense, it is like the idea of a self, although in many people's minds, the soul is a more abstract, intangible self. Nevertheless, we can ask: does the soul refer to a small self or a big self … or is it more complicated than that?

At first glance, since we speak of individual souls and of having a soul, it would seem that the soul is a kind of small self. However, it is sometimes said to be immortal, which suggests a connection to a larger self. But again, it is sometimes said to be created, which suggests it can be destroyed. It is often conceived as something that is pure, but which can also be corrupted or twisted.

Some traditions maintain that only humans have souls. Others say animals have souls as well. Still others say everything has soul, even rocks, trees, rivers, and wind. If we start to get into all the different ways this word could be used, the variations become overwhelming. Nobody, it seems, has nailed down what a soul is. And we should not expect to do so here.

The soul is likely an idea that goes way back into prehistory. Similar words exist in a variety of languages. In the Proto-Indo-European language family, they can be traced back to a word meaning "to breathe." At the most basic level, the soul is the breath of life. It is the *anima,* the essence, the animating principle of being. When our ancestors wondered at their existence — at their births, their lives, and their deaths — they tried to make sense of it in terms of a "soul."

Every variation possible has probably been explored by one tradition or another. Some have said there are two souls or even seven souls. Sometimes the soul takes on seemingly contradictory characteristics. But invariably the soul somehow represents the self. Insofar as the soul is identified with an individual, with a finite existence, with corruptibility, sin, or delusion, it points to the small self. Insofar as the soul is identified with a transcendent, unlimited, immortal, infinite being, it points to the big self. But one way or another, it is a marker of existential identity.

In this way, the word *soul,* like the word *self,* can shape aspects of itself to different meanings, large and small, depending on usage. Whether the soul is real or unreal, illusory or transcendent, mortal or immortal, depends entirely on how the word is used. Whatever the case, any individual soul always stands in relation to something larger than itself, generally God, the creator. And it is to this larger being — to its source — that the soul strives to return. Reunion with God is the ultimate end of all souls.

Ego and Self

Ego is a word that, as far as I can tell, is always used to refer to the small self. Finally a word without any ambiguity about whether it is big or small! Nobody ever talks about the divine ego, the true ego, or being-ego-bliss. The word just doesn't have any higher aspirations. It is content to be the mundane, conventional, personal, limited, individual self. A person's ego, with all its desires and aversions, hopes and fears, beliefs and conditioning, is at times a comfort and at times a tyrant, at times magnanimous and at times petty, but it is never transcendent. Nobody ever speaks of the transcendent ego. The ego is always something to be transcended.

The ego is differentiated from the idea of the small self and personal soul through its use as a psychological concept. It is therefore more concerned with memory, preference, behavior, personality, and so on than with any kind of individual essence. However, in general conceptualization it differs very little. In the dominant worldview, the idea of an individual soul has simply been replaced with the idea of the ego and rooted in materialistic theories of body and brain-centered consciousness. But it is still simply a concept of the individual self. That part has not changed.

In any case, a lot of confusion still arises from this word, *ego*. Some of the confusion comes from a psychological term being used in a spiritual context. And some of it comes from spiritual advice regarding what to do about this whole ego thing.

In the psychological realm, the ego is said to balance the passions of the id and cultural conditioning of the super-ego. In a larger sense, the ego could be said to contain both id and super-ego. Thus simplifying the matter, we can just talk about the ego as a whole. But if we stick with this psychological usage, there doesn't seem to be a higher, truer, or bigger self to attain or realize. While the atman may be realized as Brahman and the soul may be reunited with God, the ego can only look forward to a better balance … or to death.

In spiritual discourse, the ego is often seen as an obstacle, representing a false self, which must be done away with in order for enlightenment to occur. Because the spiritual aspirant is identified with the ego, to go beyond it or to do away with it may indeed seem like death or annihilation. Hence the difficulty of going beyond, especially since the psychological model does not point to a higher truth or a bigger self.

In the most aggressive discourse, aspirants are encouraged to *kill* the ego, thereby bringing about some realization of what lies beyond. But such talk can lead to deeper confusion. It is potentially misguided, even potentially harmful. By all means restrain the ego, even to the point of being *like* death, but don't heap ignorance onto ignorance. Don't put the cart before the horse. Investigate! Find out what the ego is, before you kill it. Then, at least, you would know *how* to kill it. But having truly found out, I can assure you, no killing will be necessary. For if the ego is a false self, there is nothing to kill. Realize the true self and the problem of the ego will be left behind. You will find yourself already beyond.

What, then, is that true self the psychological model fails to point toward? It is none other than reality itself. For the ego appears in the mind, and the mind appears in reality, and being in reality it is nothing but reality itself. That is the big self that lies beyond the small self of the ego. It is a reality that is all encompassing, without qualification, and without limitation. It is a reality that cannot be known except through realization, that cannot be seen except through being. So while it is not necessary to kill the ego — its life and death will take care of itself — going beyond is still a matter of going beyond.

MIND, NO MIND, AND MIND ONLY

Many people identify themselves with something called a mind. What this mind is, other than the experience of themselves, is never quite clear. The brain is often identified with the mind and the mind with the self, such that some will say they *are* their brain ... or perhaps their central nervous system. Alternately, the mind is sometimes taken to be a part of the self, as in "mind and body" or "mind, body, and spirit." In either case, the mind is considered to be composed of thoughts and memories, the personality, behavior patterns, and all mental processes. Therefore, identification with the individual mind is another example of the small self.

There should be no big mystery here. By now we are familiar with the pattern of small self and big self. As we might expect, we find in the spiritual literature mention of *small mind* and *big mind*, also of *monkey mind, no mind,* and *mind only.* But just as each new word associated with the self brings a new way of understanding it, so it brings new confusion. That's just how it goes with words. So let's dive into this tangle of the mind.

We should first acknowledge that the various cultural and linguistic traditions treat this idea of *mind* somewhat differently. An American psychologist's idea of the mind may be quite different than an Indian philosopher's. A neuroscientist's idea may be different than a monk's. These differences are a part of the very confusion that I'm speaking of. Words are not as precise as we like to think they are. That's why philosophers spend so much time trying to define terms. Even so, people from many varied traditions agree that there *is* a mind and talk about it as that thing that makes all our mental functions work.

The small mind is just what we generally consider the ordinary mind. It is the everyday mind, the intellectual mind, and the neurotic mind. It represents the mental processes of an individual's internal life. It is considered separate from the objects of perception, from other beings, and from the outside world which it perceives. It is the mind that measures and judges, names and conceptualizes, chooses and assigns credit. The ordinary mind is the mind most of us are identified with, and it is a mind that doles out desire and suffering in equal measure.

It may seem as if we are trapped within the ordinary mind, except for brief moments between thoughts or in deep sleep — between ordinary mind identification — when we can catch a little glimpse of *no mind.* This *no mind,* however, is just not the ordinary mind. It is a fleeting taste of that which is beyond the ordinary mind, but because we are still identified with the ordinary mind, it does not last, and we cannot know its depths.

Eventually we may consider that *everything* perceived — inside *and* outside — is a function of mind. This is not really disputed by science or reason, but we keep the experience of it carefully hidden from our ordinary-mind-selves. Actual recognition of the omnipresence of mind shatters the boundaries of the small mind, revealing a big mind, a universal mind, from which nothing is excluded. This is *mind only* or *one mind.* All objects, all qualities, all perceptions, all beings, and so on, are nothing other than emanations of this one mind. This, indeed, is big self.

From this, some conclude that everything is in the mind. But there is one more step to take. Mind itself is also an object within the mind! If every *thing* is in the mind, then mind also is in that. And because I *am* that, I say mind itself is an illusion.

Consciousness, Unconsciousness, and Consciousness Itself

To address *consciousness,* we must account for the many different ways the word is used in everyday and spiritual language. There are, apparently, various kinds or levels of consciousness, as well as unconsciousness and consciousness itself. We'll have to look into all these if we are to unravel some of the confusion surrounding this word. But let's start by saying that on some level, in some way, regardless of usage, we often imagine our identity as being tied to consciousness.

In the spiritual discourse, and in science too, there is a lot of confusion about consciousness and what it is. That's simply because nobody really *knows* what consciousness is. To hide this great mystery, we speak the word with confidence. We apply it to various circumstances as if we knew what it was, when in reality we do not know what it is. Hence all the confusion.

What one person calls consciousness another calls awareness, another calls being awake, and another calls the mind. In everyday usage, people say you are conscious when awake and unconscious when asleep. How about when dreaming? Well, it depends who you ask. Some will say you are only sometimes conscious when dreaming. Some will say you are always unconscious when dreaming. Others will say you are always conscious when dreaming. Most will say you are definitely unconscious in deep sleep, but those who point to pure consciousness dispute it, saying there is never any interruption in consciousness.

Is consciousness intermittent or constant? This question is key to figuring out what kind of consciousness we're talking about. For consciousness too falls into the familiar pattern, with a small version and a big version. And whether we imagine consciousness as being intermittent or constant is a clue to whether we are talking about a small consciousness or a big consciousness.

Any version of consciousness that comes and goes points toward the small self, the ego, the individual mind, and so on. This ego-awareness type of consciousness disappears in deep sleep, and may or may not be present when dreaming. Even while awake, it drifts in and out. When it's present, we say we're conscious; when it's not present, we say we're unconscious.

What does the individual consciousness come and go *in?* From where does it arise? Into what does it disappear? And can we ever be aware of or remember a time when we were unconscious? If we are aware of or remember being unconsciousness, is that not consciousness? And if are never aware of being unconscious, why even give credence to the notion? These are all good questions for investigating the nature of big consciousness.

Any version of consciousness that is always present, through all states and experiences, without limitation, points toward the big, universal self. It is that in which the small consciousness of waking, dreaming, and sleeping appears and disappears. This big consciousness is not possessed by any subject or object, but is that in which all subjects and objects appear and disappear. It is consciousness itself … or consciousness without subjects or objects.

Any notion of expanding consciousness or experiencing higher levels of consciousness always relate to small consciousness and the small self. That is not to say consciousness-expanding practices or experiences of different levels of consciousness are not helpful in realizing universal consciousness. They are. But consciousness itself cannot be expanded, nor be broken into levels, for it is without limitation or distinction. Only limited consciousness can be expanded. Only low-level consciousness can experience a higher level. Only a particular type of consciousness can experience a different type. It is the contrast between the various things — sensations, subjects, objects, states, and so on — arising within consciousness that allows for such experiences.

The mind and body itself — along with everything else we experience — appears in consciousness. Some posit there is a world beyond that. Others, that beyond that lies awareness or consciousness itself. Some will say there is something beyond that, God or the supreme. But all these levels, all this lexical one-upsmanship, just adds to the confusion of seekers. Perhaps *supreme* is a helpful word here, for it does not suggest anything in particular, nor any possible small version, and therefore it avoids confusion. Whatever is supreme *is* supreme. If we call it consciousness, then consciousness is all there is.

Body and Self

Let's not forget the body. There is a nearly universal association, throughout time and culture, between a particular body and the individual self. On a certain level, the body is the most basic identifier of the individual. The belief that you are your body is prevalent, regardless of any beliefs that may overlie it, such as belief in a soul. When we identify with the body, in fact, we usually do so in combination with a mind, ego, or soul element, but we should not ignore the importance of body identification itself, precisely because of how strong this belief is.

Body identification can be summarized by belief in the thought, *I am the body.* Further beliefs about body identification vary according to time and culture. These beliefs are essentially the story we tell to explain body identification. They include answers to such questions as: What is the body? What is its relationship to the world? What is its relationship to consciousness? What is its relationship to the mind? What is its relationship to God? And so on.

Beliefs about body identification usually associate the body with some other individual self concept, such as the ego, the mind, consciousness, or the soul. Then it's just a matter of how closely this concept is linked to the body. Sometimes it's directly linked such that ego, mind, or consciousness has the body as its source, and are therefore body dependent. Sometimes it is indirectly linked, such that the consciousness or soul resides in the body or is trapped in the body, but is not wholly body dependent. In other words, it has its source elsewhere. There are a lot of variations and mash-ups, but body identification beliefs tend to fall somewhere within these general types.

Clearly, even if the individual self is imagined as the ego or the mind, when that self is dependent on the body, there is body identification. If the mind is a function of brain activity, for example, to think you are your mind is to think you are your body. Furthermore, even when the individual self is imagined to be independent of the body, there is still body identification. That's why we call it *my* body.

So whether beliefs tend toward seeing the body as synonymous with the self or just inextricably linked to the self, there is a strong sense of body identification. And insofar as we identify with an individual body, it is a rather small kind of self. It is born, it ages, it gets injured, it gets sick, and it dies. It needs regular attention or it will dehydrate or starve. It gets tired and falls asleep. It is filled with seemingly insatiable desires, yet is limited with regard to space and time.

Of course, since the body is usually associated with another idea of self — like a soul, ego, mind, or consciousness — the big self which lies beyond the small body self can certainly appear as God, as reality itself, as a universal mind, or as consciousness itself. But it should be no surprise by now to find in the spiritual literature a kind of big body self as well. We find this big body appearing in Jewish mysticism as the body of God, in Christianity as the body of Christ, in Buddhism as the truth body, and so on. The idea that the ultimate being has a body may seem strange to us, but it's there in the mystical traditions.

Reality can be imagined as a single unified body of being that is the unbounded, limitless self. To realize this great body of being, we must dispel the belief that we are a small body. We should directly examine our experience of the physical body, all its sensations and operations, in greater and greater detail, to determine what *is* self and what *is not* self. When our idea of a self cannot be found in any part or experience of the body, nor in the body as a whole, we may have insight into the great body of being. And when belief that we are the physical body is fully dispelled, small body identification will cease. Then only the boundless, limitless body will remain.

Can there be Two Selves?

Now may be a good time to remind you of what we said in the beginning: that we would *deliberately* throw ourselves into the tangles. If you're confused at this point about the question of identity, or any other question with regard to spirituality, don't worry. Keep reading, with the assurance that no matter how confused you may feel, the clarity you seek is always at hand. The confusion itself is only a thought about a tangle of other thoughts.

We have looked at the little self and the big self and various forms they take within different traditions and different systems of thought. We have considered the apparent self and non-self, atman and paramatman. We have considered the ego and reality itself, consciousness and consciousness itself, the soul and God, the spirit and the great spirit, the mind and mind-only, the body and the universe. How many selves can there be?

Conceptually, all these various terms are talking about different things. Conceptually, an ego is not a soul, and reality is not non-self. They are different concepts, for sure. But nevertheless, as we said early on in the chapter, again and again we see the pattern of a kind of small self that represents the individual, egoic, body-bound self ... and a big self that represents a boundless, universal, all-encompassing self.

It is tempting, therefore, to say there must be two selves ... or two levels of our identity. The whole point of spirituality, we may say, is to realize our higher self ... or to expand consciousness until it merges with and embodies the greater self. This is not a bad idea.

It's a good place to start, but it is only a starting place and not the end of the spiritual path — nor of our inquiry. Insofar as it goes, it is still only an idea, and not ... how shall I say it ... reality itself *itself*.

We talk of the small self and the big Self, but can there be two selves? How can there be? Who is aware of the small self? If the small self realizes the big self, who is aware of that? Is not the self who is aware, aware of both? Is there not a self beyond both small and big self? Again, can there be two selves?

For example, perhaps you say you don't trust yourself. Well ... who says so? Do you trust that self? Is the "self" that you don't trust really the self? This is an important question. What is the self that you don't trust?

Look to the one who is aware of self, the one who says, "I am." Generally, we don't see it because we *are* it. If we don't turn the eye of the self on itself, we project the self onto various conceptual things, onto egos and souls, bodies and universes ... and concepts of God, consciousness, and reality. But if we realize this "I am" without jumping to "I am this" or "I am that," then the boundary between small self and big self falls away, and we discover that which we truly are. The actual self — beyond all concepts — encompasses all other selves.

Metaphorically speaking, we cannot see the forest for the trees. All we are doing by coming up with concepts of the self is covering up the reality of the self. We are mistaking a finger for the moon. I said earlier that "you should resolve to find out for yourself what the self is, so that you will know at last what to let go of and what to abide in when the times comes." But in reality, when you really find out what the self is, you have already let go.

In the end, there is nothing but the Self. Whatever you want to call it — self, no-self, consciousness, God, et cetera — beyond words and concepts, there has never been anything but that.

3

THE WORLD QUESTION

I turned my gaze
toward the rising moon,
and forgot all else.
Self, gaze, and world —
All gone.

Confusion About the World

As far as spirituality goes, the question of the world is almost as big as the question of identity. Depending on the tradition, sometimes it's even bigger. Either way, spiritual systems often incorporate some explanation of the world we live in, as well as other worlds, heavenly realms, hell realms, spirit dimensions, and so on. What are we to make of them?

Most people are more sure about the world than they are about themselves. You would think it would be the other way around. But, they say, what could be more concrete, more taken for granted, or more undeniably real than the world around us? It is there for all to see, touch, taste, feel, and hear. Who could deny such a manifest reality? And yet … what is it? We rarely ask this question. Instead, we rest in the various assumptions we have about the world and what others have told us about it.

Nowadays, the question of the world is mainly framed by scientific explanations. In previous times, it had been explained by religious worldviews and traditional cosmologies. Of course, some of those views and cosmologies still exist today, in part or in whole, alongside the dominant scientific explanations. And ultimately, most people's worldviews are a fluid amalgam of old and new ideas.

Confusion about the world runs deep … mainly because its fundamental mystery is so well hidden from ourselves. We are so resolute in maintaining that we are not confused by it, that we understand what is happening, that the appearance of the world is not an astonishing miracle, that we rarely question our experience. We are so comforted by our conception of the world — whatever it may be — that we rarely confront the mystery right in front of our eyes. Instead, we convince ourselves completely that our conception of the world is the same as what we see. Then our experience becomes a complete confirmation of our thought-based worldview.

Mystical teachings challenge traditional views of the world. The world is an illusion, they say. The truth does not lie in appearances, but behind and within all appearances. All diversity and multiplicity is a myth. Life is like a dream. The kingdom of heaven is spread upon the earth. There are no objects, no subjects, and no events. This world, as we conceive of it, is unreal. God alone is real.

Such teachings point to a reality beyond the world we imagine. Like various conceptions of the self, they seem to suggest a false world and a true world. Let's face it — if not fully investigated — this is just another worldview, in which we profess disbelief of the present world in favor of imagining some truer world beyond. But such teachings are doing more than simply offering another worldview. They are pointing toward a truth that is beyond all worldviews.

To expose and resolve the confusion about the world — to unravel its mystery — will require something far more radical than simply adopting a new worldview. So let's delve into various ideas that relate to the world, and see where they take us.

THE WORLD AS ILLUSION

Unfortunately, many people today dismiss the mystical teachings when they hear things like "The world is illusion," or "The experience of the world is like a dream." The materialist worldview that dominates so many minds precludes serious consideration of such statements. We are so certain that our experience of the world is real that we do not view it as *willful* certainty. So when the spiritual teachings proclaim that the world is unreal, it runs counter to everything we imagine our experience to be.

Often the seeker becomes hung up on words like "unreal" or "delusion" or "dream" without really understanding them. This is to be expected, but it's helpful to remind ourselves that we do not fully understand. Then, rather than simple dismissal, we can entertain a deeper investigation, even if we remain skeptical. So forget about real and unreal. There is the world. It's right before your eyes. But what is its true nature? Find that out, and all the talk of real and unreal will be resolved.

It's important to note that these teachings are not an anomaly and not limited to one tradition, religion, or culture. Although the face of this illusion has become the concept of *maya* found in the Hindu and Buddhist traditions, the teaching that the truth is not what it seems — that there is more to reality than meets the eye or the mind — is incredibly widespread, if not universal among mystical traditions. From shamanic lore to modern mystical theologies, all speak of a truth beyond this world.

Furthermore, the testimonies of true mystics are not assertions of mere belief, but rather statements of direct experience. I can attest to this, for I too once dismissed such teachings as far-fetched and speculative at best. But I am now speaking from direct experience, rather than cleverly-hidden speculation. Such a change can be likened to the story of the apostle Paul, who persecuted the Christians until he encountered the resurrected Christ. From then on, he spoke with a power that came not from himself, but from this higher power which he had encountered.

When we're told that what we have defined in our minds as real is unreal, and what seems impossible is the true reality, objections should not be surprising. That is the rational mind at work, and on some level is commendable. But ignorance — and the illusion of the world — lies in how the mind hides its own work from itself. We ourselves construct the apparent solidity and "reality" of the world through layer upon layer of dream-like imaginings, covering our tracks as we go. So when viewing the painting, we no longer see the pencil lines, the pencil, or our own hand in its creation.

The world as illusion is not a teaching that points toward some conspiracy against the self. It is the very work and magic of the self. It is not a trick that is being played upon you by some external force. It *is* you. When you recognize that completely, the veil of the individual ego-self is lifted. Then you too will know what is meant by the *illusion* of the world.

MANY WORLDS ONE TRUTH

With regard to the nature of the world, one of the issues that arises is which world we are talking about. Is it the physical world? The mental world? The collective world? The personal world? The objective world? When it comes down to it, there seem to be so many worlds. How could we ever keep them straight or come to any conclusions about this world?

At the outset, as usual, it may seem obvious. We're talking about *the* world, this world, or the material world, and we are all talking about the same world. But if we begin to examine — just a little bit — this word "world," suddenly we're not so sure. Maybe the world you're experiencing is slightly different, or even radically different than the world I am experiencing.

Our idea of the material world is, roughly speaking, that the world that appears in our consciousness is an objective reality made of stuff that is separate and independent from our consciousness. Although there's no proof for this idea, we take it on faith because it seems to work well as a model for going about our business. But accepting this widely-accepted idea means there are at least two worlds, the world appearing in the mind and the material world. Ideally we imagine that the mind world accurately reflects the material world — and we act as if it does — even though we know from experience they don't always match up.

But that's just the tip of the iceberg. Given this material model, we also know that the mind world only represents a narrow spectrum of material-world phenomena. We can see, hear, taste, smell, and feel … but only in a narrow band of visible light, audible frequency, and so on. So even if we take our mind world to be fairly accurate, what we experience is only one limited possibility. The experiential world of a dog or a bat must be radically different from the world of a person. And so there must exist worlds of experience that are entirely beyond our ability to imagine.

Going further, we must recognize that the mind world represented in each separate mind is also a unique view of the material world — and so in some sense is also a different world. Even if each mind is representing an objective world in a similar way, each mind sees that world from a different vantage point. So every person that has ever lived has experienced a different world, a unique world shaped by their view, their experiences, their thoughts, their feelings.

With so many possible worlds, it's no wonder we seek solace and simplicity in the idea of an objective world, independent of consciousness and unaffected by minds. To imagine everyone's experience being so different can be overwhelming. It can feel alienating, confusing, and isolating. One can start to feel trapped in one's mind, unable to ever truly experience what we think is the "real" world. And there are a number of dangers in this area that could lead one further into delusion, and into immoral or even psychotic behavior.

So what are we to do? We are lost in our own world and in a multitude of other worlds. The path lies in recognizing the mistakes we have made, in seeing what we have left out, and revealing how we have tricked ourselves into our current beliefs. The path lies in folding the mind into the world and the world into the mind. Then we can see clearly that mind and world arise together, and the source of both is one and the same.

The objective world that we imagine is itself a part of the mind world. In other words, the material world is only an idea — as is the mind and body, and any other world we might imagine. Drop all these ideas, and only the truth will remain.

Supernatural Realms

Many of our spiritual convictions, whatever they may be, hinge on the belief in supernatural realms. Think about it. *This* world we take for granted, but we imagine the spiritual dimensions to be elevated or other-worldly. We speak of heavens and hells, astral planes and cosmic voids, purgatories and in-between realms. And in these places a host of spiritual beings reside: Buddhas and enlightened masters, angels and disembodied spirits, ghosts and demons, gods and devas, and of course the supreme God.

The chief characteristic of these realms seems to be that they are elsewhere. They are not of *this* world. They are distinct and separate from this world. But they can be reached through special states, through visions, through divine grace, or through death. But are they real? That's the question many would like an answer to. Or are they just the product of our imagination, combined with our worldly hopes and fears?

That's a reasonable question. For most people, it just comes down to faith in their worldview. If we hold a belief that at least some kind of supernatural realms exist — heaven, hell, astral planes, et cetera — we will accept their existence and interpret any extraordinary experience as possible confirmation that they do exist. If we hold a belief that supernatural realms do not exist — that they are a product of the imagination — then we will reject their existence and interpret our experiences, be they normal or extraordinary, according to that view. Of course, some withhold judgment, but they are still looking for judgment on the matter, as if waiting for sufficient accumulation of evidence, one way or the other.

The most important thing is this: with all our views, we are getting ahead of ourselves. Here is how to check. Do we understand the nature of the world that appears before us right now? Do we know what it is and why it appears? Do we understand the observer of this world? If we have not investigated these things thoroughly and come to deep understanding, how can we expect to understand the nature of the supernatural world.

Of course, continue your spiritual practice, whatever it is, but stop trying to grasp at what you think is true or untrue. Stop judging or withholding judgment. The truth is not hidden by anything or anyone other than yourself, by the ego or the mind, which holds itself separate from the world, and so sees the world, and all worlds, as separate and limited. It is natural, then, for the ego-self to accept or reject various worlds based on how it perceives and judges those limitations. Thus we deem various supernatural realms to be real or unreal based on our view.

To illustrate, let us consider the dream world. While in a dream, we generally treat the dream world as real. In the waking world we treat it as unreal. But both the dream world and the waking world consist of sights, sounds, sensations, thoughts, emotions, and so on. Both experiences can be seen as mind worlds. Sleeping or waking, both are mind, real or unreal according only to your desires, your hopes, your fears — your view.

Some have seen the throne of God. And some have been touched by angels of the Lord. Some have felt the fires of hell. And some have been tempted by demons. Some have seen the departed appear before them. And some have been given council by spirit-beings. So let me be clear: the supernatural realms are as real and as tangible as whatever realm you see before you now. But the presence of one realm may make other realms appear less real. For example, while in a hell realm one cannot imagine the peace of a heavenly realm, but when there, the peace is clearly felt.

All realms are experienced as mind worlds. See what is beyond the present mind, and you will see what is behind all realms, just as you will see what lies behind all states, the natural and the supernatural.

What Matters

I have a friend who is a physicist. Beyond the basic (for a physicist) credentials, he's also a deep thinker and seeker of ultimate truth. One day, thinking to probe the mysteries of the physical world, I asked him, "What is matter?"

He said, "Well, as physicists we have a standard answer, but I'm guessing that's not what you mean."

"No, I mean, when it gets right down to it, what *is* it?"

Without hesitation, he said "Oh, we don't know." He went on to say that while we can observe the various properties of matter and so on, we don't *really* know what it is. "Although we have learned a lot," he said, "we don't fundamentally know what matter is … or what space is, either."

The work of physics starts with some assumptions that aren't really known, and proceeds from there. Some scientists, like my friend, may keep these assumptions and the big fundamental unknowns in mind, but that's not always the case. Sometimes they just forget about that stuff so they can get on with their work, looking at data, crunching numbers, and so on. And sometimes, especially in fields other than physics, they've never even considered these fundamental underlying assumptions.

This *not knowing* probably goes even deeper than you imagine. We might imagine that, like other questions, we just need a little more information and we'll be able to say what something is. But while it's certainly possible that we could learn more and say more based on our observations, such developments would inevitably raise questions of their own.

Could we ever really be able to answer a question such as, "What is reality itself?" One would need some perspective, but we cannot get outside of reality to say what it is or isn't. Wherever one goes there is just reality. And whatever one experiences, it is just the observing mind, and that too is just reality itself. So it can't be anything in particular — anything that could be distinguished from something else.

The history of investigating matter has been a succession of ideas and ever-more-minute observations, from cells to molecules to atoms to electrons, and has revealed some stunning results regarding our ability to manipulate matter for various effects, be they atomic explosions, supercomputers, or microwave ovens. Nobody can say these effects don't happen, and yet the true nature of matter eludes us. And so the true nature of the physical world also eludes us.

My physicist friend recently noted that he had been thoughtfully musing about the nature of atoms. He said, "Either an atom is essentially nothing … or everything. Maybe it's more accurate to say it's either nowhere or everywhere. By that I mean, the standard model of the atom is made of elementary particles, so if we consider an elementary particle like an electron, it is commonly thought of as a zero-dimensional-point particle that has a probability field describing its position that extends throughout all of existence."

I found this line of thinking quite interesting. From a spiritual perspective, what matters is not individual particles, events, and various things, but all of existence and non-existence — everything and nothing. Whatever material object you may consider, if you relentlessly investigate its limits, it will eventually lead you to everything and nothing.

Matter and space are only ideas. They're useful concepts when explaining the various phenomena of our experience. As thoughts, they form the backbone of a functional model that helps us go about our activity. Whatever we might decide matter is or is not, that will still be only an idea. Space, consciousness, the mind, and so on are also the same. Even reality could be said to be only an idea. But if we discard all these ideas, what remains is the great mystery of being — and to that we can only point with a myriad of names.

Beginnings and Endings

What is the beginning and end of the world? Again, it depends on what world we're talking about: the physical world, the mental world, the earth, the universe, your world, my world, et cetera. All the worlds that we can talk about are thought-created worlds, and they may begin and end at different points.

We imagine the physical universe coming into being at some point in the distant past and speculate about its end at some point in the distant future. Well, what happened before that and what will happen after that? Some say time itself comes into being with the physical universe, so there is not a before or after. Some say there was or will be another physical universe.

Our individual mental world starts sometime in childhood, when we begin to make distinctions between ourselves and the world. We identify with the body and with our thoughts, our mind, and we begin to live in that world of the individual. Although our mental world starts in childhood, because it identifies with the body, we imagine its beginning goes back to a physical birth. We then fear death as the end of this world. And we are troubled by other potential or partial endings such as insanity or dementia, through which we imagine our personal world may become so unrecognizable as to be essentially ended.

The world of the earth, the world of life on earth, the world of humanity, and the world of the individual are all different worlds. Each world has its imagined beginning and its imagined ending. And each world has a story associated with it, with recalled or recovered past events and potential future events.

The only world that is unaccounted for is the world as it is, now. It is the only world within our direct experience. It is the only real world. It is the only world you can ever be sure of. And yet we almost completely ignore it, substituting for it various thought-created worlds, imagined beginnings and imagined endings.

The world that we directly experience always begins now and always ends now. Always beginning, always ending, it is without either. Fall into this world — surrender to it — and you will find a world without beginning ... and a world without end.

Relative and Absolute

The idea that there is the relative truth and an absolute truth is woven throughout many spiritual traditions. This idea may take various forms, but they all reflect the same dualistic idea. We can look at this idea as suggesting there are two worlds: a relative world and an absolute world.

What we think of as the world is some form of the relative truth. In other words, the relative truths of the world are conditional. We might say something exists, like a tree, but it only exists for period of time, outside of which it does not exist. It exists in one place and not another place. It exists when a mind sees it as a tree. And so on. Thus, it cannot be said to absolutely exist.

On the other hand, the absolute truth is not conditional. It's hard to come up with a concrete example here, because nothing we can think of is like that. There are various conceptual formulations that represent this absolute truth: God, Tao, consciousness itself, dharmakaya, and so on. People will try to draw distinctions between these, but if you look to the heart of these concepts, they are representative of an absolute truth. Any distinction made is about the concepts only, which are conditional, but the words ultimately point to the unconditional.

The Upanishads speak of *Brahman*. It's a beautiful conceptual formulation of the absolute. Brahman is the ultimate reality. It is all pervasive, infinite, and eternal. It is without beginning and without end. It is the changeless source of all that is, and into it all things subside. What's great about Brahman is that it's very hard to mistake it for anything relative. It is the supreme, the absolute truth, and it is not complicated much by images, qualities, and further concepts.

One of the challenges for seekers in the West is that God has been given so many worldly representations that it's easy to mistake these representations for God. In doing so, we risk worshiping something in the relative world. This is a path to idolatry. But the line is subtle, for the relative and absolute, the world and God, are not separate. The absolute is absolute, and all relative worlds cannot be separate from that. So God is present even in worldly things. God is the underlying truth behind everything.

When Christians regard bread and wine as the body and blood of Christ, they are, ideally, not worshipping material things. They are acknowledging that the reality of God is truly in everything. They have the doctrine of transubstantiation to explain how ordinary bread and wine becomes Christ's real presence. But the truth is that Christ is never absent and that God's reality permeates all things.

In the Buddhist tradition, the unity of the relative and the absolute is expressed in the Heart Sutra: "Form is emptiness, and emptiness is form." The multitude of various forms that make up the world are empty — empty of essence, empty of self, empty of existence. But this emptiness appears as the diversity of forms that compose this world.

It is said that Brahman is one, without second. The sages have declared: The world is unreal; Brahman alone is real. But also that the world *is* Brahman, or the appearance of Brahman. Some are confused by the statement that the world is unreal. Certainly it appears before you, but it's not what you think. The relative world — and even the individual self — are appearances of a fundamental reality that is itself beyond all appearances. So here too, we see that the world is nothing other than a manifestation of the supreme reality. And indeed, how could it be anything but that?

THE UNIVERSE AND REALITY

Nowadays when we think of the world, many either think about Earth or the universe. When thinking about just the Earth, we still acknowledge that it exists in the larger world of the whole universe. And the universe we imagine as all of space, along with everything and all phenomena in it. Because we understand everything in terms of things — objects and events — we try to understand the universe as an object or an event, attempting to define its edges and limits, its beginning and end.

Our efforts to define the universe can lead to confusion about how to imagine the universe. On the one hand, we would like to say the universe is everything that's out there. The word implies "one," "whole," or "everything all together." On the other hand, that kind of infinite possibility does not sit well with the mind. Because we struggle to understand the universe as an object or an event, we look for its limits. When we find limits, the questions come: What's beyond that? What happened before that? And so on. Some people now like to speculate about a multiverse. But that's just another way of saying what we thought was the universe wasn't really everything.

We tend to think of the universe as somehow fundamental. But there is something more fundamental than the universe ... something more real than the universe. And that is reality itself. It's not space, but space appears in it. It's not time, but time appears in it. It's not matter, or energy, or spirit. But all these arise within, or upon, or from ... reality itself. *What* is it? Nobody can say, because it has no limits — no beginning, no end, no dimension, no edge, no inside, no outside, no volume, no boundary. But it is more real than a hundred billion galaxies.

Our understanding of the universe changes over time. A mere hundred years ago, we didn't know galaxies existed outside our own. Five hundred years before that, again, our picture of the universe was very different. From year to year, from culture to culture, our understanding of the phenomenal world varies continuously. In our own experience, our picture of the world when we are a child is different from our picture of the world as an adult. Even as an adult, our picture of the world may change many times. And, of course, our vantage point, our view, our sense-perceptions are also always changing.

Reality itself is always the same. You may recognize it or ignore it, but it never varies, never comes, never goes. It does not expand or contract or age. This diamond-like reality is without limits, encompassing everything that ever was, is, or will be. And it is always here and now.

In our quest to understand the world, again and again we are presented with this same seemingly dualistic story. The unreal and the real, the relative and the absolute, the universe and reality itself, the world and Brahman. All this seems to suggest there are two worlds, except that in each case, the one encompasses the other, and the other appears in the one.

THE ONE WORLD

Perhaps the strongest arguments made on behalf of the world is that we can see it, hear it, touch it, taste it, smell it, and so on. Some might even define the world as what can be seen, heard, touched, tasted, smelled, and so on. We can establish suitable units and measure this world, this way and that, up and down, inside and out. But what does it mean?

As an experience, the waking world is more stable than a dream, and is generally taken to be more interesting than deep sleep. And so we call the waking world *The World*. We generally consider dreams and deep sleep to be auxiliary states that support our experience in the waking world. We often ignore them, leave them out, as if sleeping and dreaming — and indeed, consciousness — were not a part of this world. But why should this be so? Doesn't the world encompass everything?

Look into your experience and see how whatever world we imagine, we imagine it by giving it boundaries. For example, we may say what we experience when we are awake is the world, while when we dream, that is not the world. It is just a dream. We may say what we can touch is the world, while what we think or imagine is not the world.

What we call the world is an aggregate of sense perceptions, coordinated and reified by the mind element, which arises within it. The world is an interplay between what is seen, seeing, and the seer. Without seeing, hearing, touching, tasting, smelling, and thinking, the world would not exist. And neither would what we think of as our self, if we imagine the self as mind and/or body.

When the waking world appears, the mind also appears, the seer of that world. It must be so, for it is the mind that discerns the world. When a dream world appears, a seer also appears. In deep sleep nothing appears, and also no mind. And yet existence permeates all three states. At no point can we deny existence.

Why put limitations on the world? Why fragment the unity of existence? Let us say the world *is* what is. When we do that, all worlds and no-world are one world. The waking worlds, the dreaming worlds, and the no-world of deep sleep are all in this one world. Sometimes various things and minds appear in this world. At other times this world is without things and without minds.

What is the one world that has no limits? If we inquire into this carefully, what we find is indistinguishable from consciousness itself, from the absolute truth, from the universal Self, and from God. It is Brahman, the supreme reality. All other worlds, all limited worlds and the minds that see them, are but appearances in this one world.

4

THE CAUSE AND EFFECT QUESTION

Without beginning or end,
Without boundary or limit,
The edges cannot hold.
Each object ... each event
Dissolves into the infinite.
Nothing really exists,
and nothing has ever happened.

Confusion About Cause and Effect

How and why do things happen? Here is another fundamental mystery that human beings have been struggling to answer. Like most of these mysteries, the various solutions take myriad forms. Here we might recognize words for fate, destiny, sin, grace, and karma as different ways we have tried to understand how and why things happen the way they do. Taken as a whole, they boil down to a relatively small constellation of related ideas which we shall here refer to as cause and effect.

Cause and effect tries to answer the question of why things happen by saying that each event is an effect of a previous cause or causes. In other words, things happen because of other things that happened. In most formulations, the cause always comes before the effect, but even that is not entirely cut and dry. Still, anything that happens is the effect of other causal events or conditions. This is something that is more or less taken for granted. But it's important to recognize that it's just an idea.

Strictly speaking, it's relatively easy to say this thing happened after another thing, or certain things usually happen when certain other things happen. It's somewhat more of a stretch to say that one thing *caused* the other thing. I'm not trying to tell you how things are — you have to look into it — but this whole idea of causation is not as iron-clad as we like to think it is. It relies on a series of concepts and presuppositions that cannot be entirely grounded. While some form of cause and effect may appear to be the law of the land, appearances can be misleading.

From a spiritual perspective, this is important because, ultimately, we are not seeking just a workable model. We are seeking the absolute truth. We are interested in seeing beyond mere appearances, whatever they may be. But everywhere we look, the idea of causes and causation is in question or in conflict. Free will exists seemingly outside of causation on the one hand and of God's omnipotence on the other. Karma keeps us bound and yet somehow leads us to liberation. Sin separates us from God, and yet God's mercy and love are infinite. We view physical events as deterministic on one level, but probabilistic on another level. We say things have definite causes, and yet we can never really track them all down.

There is a lot of confusion about cause and effect. What's really going on here? Why do things happen the way they happen? We do not have consistent answers. In fact, this is another example of how we are constantly shifting our ideas around, subtly taking this view or that view in order to make sense of things, and to keep us from looking directly into the heart of mystery.

A WILD FOX TALE

There is no better way to throw ourselves into the tangle of cause and effect than by recounting the tale of Baizhang and the Wild Fox. This perplexing Zen koan is all the more perplexing because of cultural nuance, supernatural elements, and translation difficulties. It's a story set in a world far removed from our own, and yet it strikes at the heart of our confusion about cause and effect. And it's a pretty amusing tale as well. I've read a couple different versions and am going by memory here, so bear with me.

Whenever the monk Baizhang was giving his morning talk, a strange old man showed up and stood at the back. One morning, after almost everybody had left, the old man approached.

"Who are you?" Baizhang asked, suspecting the old man was a ghost.

The old man said, "I was the head monk a very long time ago on this very mountain, but I am not actually a man anymore. A student once asked me if an enlightened person falls into cause and effect. I said 'No,' and because of that, I was transformed into a wild fox for 500 lifetimes."

The old man requested that Baizhang give him some words of wisdom that would free him from his wild-fox body, and then he asked, "Does an enlightened person fall into cause and effect?"

Baizhang said, "Don't ignore cause and effect."

The old man was awakened instantly and confirmed that he had indeed been freed from being a wild fox. He asked to be given a monk's funeral, saying "I will be in the mountain behind the monastery." Then he departed.

Baizhang led the other monks up the mountainside behind the monastery. They found a dead fox in the entrance to a cave, and they gave it a proper monk's funeral.

Later, one of Baizhang's students asked him what that was all about. Baizhang told him the story of the old man who was turned into a wild fox after denying that an enlightened person falls into cause and effect.

The student asked, "What if he hadn't said 'No'?"

Baizhang said, "Come here, and I'll show you."

The student approached Baizhang, but before Baizhang could slap the student, the student slapped him.

Baizhang laughed and clapped his hands. He said, "I thought only barbarians have red beards, but it appears you have one too."

Okay — can we just pause for moment as modern readers and acknowledge how wonderfully bonkers this story is. I can't love it enough! It has everything: ghosts, supernatural foxes, mountain temples, reincarnation, caves, Zen monks, enlightenment, maybe doppelgangers, maybe time travel — and of course, cause and effect. It starts so mundanely with an old guy standing at the back of a lecture, and then it just gets weirder and weirder.

And really, that's not even all. Hitting the books and the internet, I found a few elements I left out or misremembered, and translation variants that give different angles on the whole encounter.

First, we should note that Baizhang is called Hyakujo in the Japanese tradition, and appears that way in many translations. The fox's den is actually on the *other* side of the mountain, not just up the mountain as in my account. In some versions, the old man disappears after talking with Baizhang, perhaps showing that he is, indeed, a ghost. Baizhang's talk with his students happens in an assembly of all the monks, and sometimes the student asks, "What if the monk had answered correctly?" And, of course, Baizhang's comment about barbarians is a reference to Bodhidharma, as if to tell his student, "Nice one!"

In Senzaki's translation, Baizhang's answer is "The enlightened man is one with the law of causation," which is a little more clear, but not as subtle. In Yamada's translation, Baizhang says "The law of causation cannot be obscured." Which again is kind of the same, but different. I'm sure there are other variations.

And finally, there are interesting contextual tidbits. As a head monk, Baizhang would have been named after the mountain where the monastery was. Since the old man was also a master on that mountain, he too would have been called Baizhang. And in Chinese mythology, a fox could be a devious trickster, or even an evil spirit, so there is a hint of darkness to the old man's fate of being reborn as a wild fox for 500 lifetimes and in his appearance before Baizhang.

In the tangles yet? We haven't even gotten into Wumen's commentary, which asks why the old man's answer leads to him being transformed into a wild fox, and why does Baizhang's answer free him. Could it possibly have something to do with cause and effect?

Let's take Wumen's word for it. I like Yamada's translation here: "If in regard to this you have the one eye, then you will understand that the former [Baizhang] enjoyed 500 lives of grace as a fox."

Spiritual Concepts

Over time and through many different traditions, spiritual discourse has offered many ideas about cause and effect. A cursory survey reveals animistic spirits, capricious gods, fate, destiny, karma, sin, divine plans, cause and effect itself, and on and on. These are all concepts related to how and why things happen. But how do we make sense of them all?

The usual way we make sense of things is pretty haphazard. We latch onto an idea because it offers answers to questions we have. How should I behave? How can I secure health and happiness for myself and my loved ones? How can I reach my ultimate potential? Many ideas may offer some measure of reassurance and potential benefit. In that sense, they are all useful ideas, so it's not surprising that they've been adopted in different guises by various traditions over the course of human history.

Usually, we are eager to adopt particular ideas as being right and reject others as being wrong, according to our individual inclinations. We want to say, for example, karma is how things work and the idea of capricious gods controlling our fates is just superstition. But all of these ideas hold some element of our experience and a particular view or model of the truth.

The spirit world points to the interconnectedness of all things and the magical feeling of experience. Capricious gods point to the seeming randomness of good and bad events. Fate and destiny point to the feeling of inevitability in every moment and to our greatest possible potential. Karma and sin point to our role in determining the course of our lives and the responsibility of our actions. The divine plan and divine will point to the largest imaginable context in which all things exist and all events happen.

These ideas do not have to be seen as potential facts to be accepted or rejected, verified or disproved. They can be seen as pieces to the puzzle of our experience, as bits of truth wrapped in language, metaphor, and imagination. This is a puzzle that is solved not by putting it together, though, but rather by taking it apart.

The present experience is a great mystery. How and why things happen is also a great mystery. We can paint this mystery with various concepts and ideas. Sometimes they are useful, guiding lights, and sometimes they are oppressive, harmful obstacles, depending on how they are adopted and put into practice. Either way, as soon as we enter the realm of concepts, we lose sight of the mystery. If instead we trace any concept we hold about how and why things happen back to its origin, we rediscover the great mystery of all existence and nonexistence.

Deep Inquiry into Cause and Effect

Cause and effect are inextricably linked to the concept of time. Without time, everything arises spontaneously *now,* and there is nowhere and no other time in which a cause could be pointed to. Without time, past and future do not exist, other than in the dreamlike imagination of the present. Because these concepts are linked, insight into one may yield insight into the other. And collapsing one, may collapse the other.

I've always liked wrist-watches. I remember listening to my dad's Seiko 5 automatic that he got when he was in Vietnam. I remember winding my first watch, although I can't remember what it looked like. In grade school, I had a digital game watch that allowed you to control a monkey who could catch coconuts falling out of two palm trees. When I was little older, I had a Casio Databank watch that could store up to 50 names and phone numbers. Eventually I settled on a Seiko quartz dive watch, which I wore for some 25 years. There's something a bit magical about these miniaturized mechanisms and their mysterious innards. Beyond their practicality and technical ingenuity, they are like subtle little koans, urging us to inquire into the nature of cause and effect.

About six month or so before my awakening, I got deep into contemplating the nature of time. In retrospect, it was not just an intellectual exercise or an idle curiosity. In my life, I felt deeply stuck, unable to move forward, unable to decide anything, and totally frustrated by being me. I was compelled, by my own suffering, to look deeply and directly into the nature of myself and the world. This inquiry into time was just a part of a larger inquiry spreading throughout my being like the rising of a tidal wave.

One day I got a *Scientific American* magazine special edition on the subject of time. I think my dad sent it to me. Inside were multiple articles on time, laying out various theories from a physics perspective. It took a sort of nobody-really-understands-time-but-here-are-some-current-ideas approach. One idea that stood out to me was an article on *block time*. In this theory, time is seen as a kind of fourth dimension through which we are moving. Imagine that all of the past and all of the future are already there, like a giant crystalline block of space-time. Everything that ever happened and everything that ever will happen already exists. You are just seeing one particular point at any given moment. There was something intriguing about this idea. It stretched my imagination beyond the bounds of how I normally experienced time. But even that wasn't enough.

At the height of this inquiry, I tried to stare into time itself. One day, sitting at my desk, forgetting all ideas, I tried to detect time directly within my perception. Slowly, I picked up a pen from one side of the desk and moved it to the other side of the desk, following it with my eyes. Then I sat for several minutes trying to fundamentally understand what had just happened. I looked at the place the pen had been and had only a memory of it being there. I looked at the place it was now, and there it was. But I could detect no passage of time! The present moment was still the present moment. *What exactly has happened?* I looked at my watch and followed the movement of the seconds hand ticking away. *What is happening?* It was like a voice calling out from deep within myself, a voice calling out for the truth of reality itself.

What is happening? Let this question ignite the sacred fire of inquiry. Accept nothing less than reality itself. Find out what is happening, and you will have no more questions about cause and effect.

BEYOND THE VELVET HORIZON

The horizon is a very interesting thing. We don't think about it much, but there it is at the limits of our vision. And beyond it … well, you can never really see beyond the horizon. That is the nature of horizons. If you travel toward it, you may see things you hadn't seen before, but you still can't see beyond the horizon.

If we look around, horizons appear again and again in various ways. The horizon is not just the line of the earth's surface in the distance; it is the limit of our senses. It's also the limit of cause and effect. Nothing beyond the horizon can really affect you. Whatever it is must somehow appear within the horizon and come into awareness.

Of course, we imagine that things are happening beyond the horizon, but we don't really have any knowledge of those things until we observe them, and when we do they are not beyond the horizon. Really, nothing ever happens beyond the horizon. For again, that is the nature of horizons.

We may experience various horizons simultaneously. For example, in darkness, the visual horizon collapses, but the auditory horizon remains or even expands. Don't be fooled by thinking that because you can have a video chat with somebody on the other side of the earth that you have somehow seen beyond the horizon. On the contrary, the person's image, their words, the video screen, and so on are all clearly on this side of the horizon. At no point have you ever seen or heard or experienced anything beyond the horizon.

Science has produced some of the most intricate and interesting horizons. Surrounding a black hole, for example, is an event horizon, beyond which nothing can escape, even light, and consequently nothing can be observed. At the center of a black hole is predicted a singularity, a place with no volume but infinite density, and any infinity, whether it appears mathematically or conceptually, is also a kind of horizon. And at the edge of the observable universe is the cosmic horizon, beyond which no light, particle or information will ever reach or affect us, due to the age of the universe, the expansion of the universe, the speed of light, and so on.

Despite vast differences in apparent scale, all horizons are really the same horizon. I said "Velvet Horizon" in the heading there just because I liked the sound of it. In any case, all the various horizons are really pointing toward the same phenomenon. It is the limit of the senses, the limit of ordinary knowledge, and the limit of cause and effect. What is the real horizon? It is the edge of the mind.

To Briefly Summarize

Causes and effects are object-events. Object-events are defined by various limitations we call time, space, and density. Usually people have no trouble seeing this. Each cause or effect is a discreet object, event, or object-event, if you will.

Object-events are all mind created. That is, the limits that define them are always created by and perceived in the mind only. This is the first place people usually get stuck. We are conditioned to believe object-events have an independent origin and existence. But if you examine your experience directly, you will never find any objects or events outside of the mind. And, in fact, the object-events arise from the mind only.

The mind itself is an object-event. It is composed of thoughts, which are also object-events. Thoughts are limited to form by other thoughts, and the mind itself falls into delusion. This is the second place people usually get stuck. Even if we are able to see object-events as arising from the mind only, we are still conditioned to believe that the mind itself is somehow separate and not an object-event itself. Again, examine your experience directly, and you will see that without the mind arising as an object-event, there is no mind whatsoever.

Beyond the mind, reality itself is limitless. Without the thoughts that limit the mind to form, the mind itself dissipates, revealing the limitless nature of reality itself. Without beginning and without end, without form or formlessness, the Self alone shines forth as pure consciousness.

In this limitless One, everything happens — minds arise, worlds appear, destinies unfold. But fundamentally, when taken as a whole, there are really no causes or effects, no object-events, no thoughts, and no mind. There is nothing separate; there is nothing at all but the limitless one.

THE GRAND ILLUSION

These are the natural questions people usually have: If there is no cause and effect, why does it seem like there is? Isn't denying cause and effect just ignoring the reality of our own experience?

Those are good questions. The short answer might be: don't deny cause and effect without going *beyond* cause of effect. In other words, it makes no sense to just say something contrary to your experience. But perhaps there is space within your experience that you have not fully explored. In any case, let's discuss this a little further.

This is a good place to slow down and take notice, because this question actually speaks to the essential difficulty so many spiritual seekers face. We believe what the teacher is saying — or at least we want to believe — but nevertheless we are not experiencing it, and we do not know it for ourselves.

I get it. I also had that experience. When I was younger and reading about enlightenment, it all sounded very good, very enticing. And it seemed to ring true somehow. But I could not get there. Sounding good and sounding true was not satisfying and did not make me happy. So for a long time, I pushed it out of my mind. I was a smart guy, I thought, so if I couldn't understand it then it must not be real. It's all pretty funny now to look back on. But it wasn't funny at the time.

We expect the truth to be particular, and to somehow be outside ourselves, separate from ourselves. But as long as we have this expectation, as long as we believe in particular things and see ourselves as separate from reality, we will fall into cause and effect. Because particular things affect other things … because the world affects us … because we affect the world … because, because, because … and effect!

Cause and effect is one of the basic hallmarks of separation. Only when we think of one entity or thing as separate from another can we even imagine cause and effect. And when, beyond our control, we believe these thoughts and imaginings are reality, then the grand illusion of multiplicity, of worlds and beings and things arises.

That is the basic situation we find ourselves in, and we will remain in this situation as long we fundamentally believe in separation. And we will continue to mistake the words with which we think and speak for the reality in which we live.

Of course, the natural follow-up is to say that we believe in separation because that is our experience.

Fair enough, but even by making such an objection, we are falling into cause and effect. It's the old chicken and egg scenario. Try to see these things in such a way that there is no difference between chickens and eggs, between yourself and the world, between your experience and your belief.

To really experience this, we must fundamentally abandon ourselves as separate beings. That is the crux of the matter and why it is so difficult for people to accept. Once done, though, we are at one with cause and effect, and so there are no causes and no effects.

IGNORANCE IS SUFFERING

Some people might be inclined to ask, "What's the point?" As if to say, "Even if there is a truth, I don't see how it's helpful," or "I don't see how the truth would benefit me."

Fair enough. I'm grateful when people speak their minds, so I know where they're coming from. But I would advise such a person to find out who it is who asks this question and makes these objections. Discover the truth for yourself first, before rushing to judgment. *Then* see if such questions or objections still arise.

Even as a point of logical argument, it's easy to see how a personal view that is inconsistent with reality can lead to suffering. We could even say that all such views inevitably lead to suffering.

And not just our own, I'll add, but the suffering of others as well. So much so that it's not a stretch to say that ignorance of the truth can be traced to the root of all suffering everywhere.

So getting to the bottom of cause and effect is of great importance, for the simple reason that our happiness depends on it. Without insight, we are tossed about in a storm of beliefs and judgments that are all at variance with the truth itself. The mind generates them, the ego identifies with them … and sooner or later suffering arises.

This is — dare I say it — just cause and effect at work. And a good thing too, because in the long run, this suffering encourages us to look deeper, to reform our ways, and to seek the truth itself, which alone can set us free.

Going Beyond Cause and Effect

Let me be clear: on a practical level, it's just foolishness to ignore cause and effect. In life, actions have consequences, and if you behave foolishly you can expect trouble. I hope you don't feel compelled to test this out too much, but I'm confident it will withstand any scrutiny. Hopefully the trouble you encounter will swiftly set you right.

There is nothing foolish, however, in asking if causes are really causes and if effects are really effects. The difference here is whether one thing actually makes another thing happen, or whether one thing just always follows the other thing, and whether there are separate things at all. For example, when a cat walks by, the head comes first and the tail comes last, but cat heads do not cause cat tails. The head and the tail, the beginning and end, go together.

Consider all of life and the whole universe as one big giant cat, sauntering by. Although some things follow other things with startling regularity, everything actually goes together. So nothing is causing anything else. Of course, another way of looking at this is that everything causes everything. Whatever you happen to be looking at, whatever is happening, it is the way it is because the whole universe is the way it is.

Even when we think about everyday occurrences, it's plain that nothing that happens has just one cause. The idea that you can pinpoint a single cause to anything is itself foolishness. The causes are multitudinous. And the effects are multitudinous. If we consider that all causes are effects themselves, and that all effects are causes of further effects, then following any branching chain of causation leads to everything, everywhere, and every-time.

Finally, when you inquire into causation, don't leave yourself out. What you think of as yourself — the mind-body-ego — is itself the effect of prior causes, and its actions are the causes of future effects. That's basic karma. Seeing the mind-body-ego as only karma in action, recognize that you are not that, but rather you are the reality, the being, in which all this takes place. Falling into cause and effect is just believing you are the mind-body-ego. Give up this belief — realize consciousness itself — and you are already beyond cause and effect.

5

THE GOD QUESTION

In the depths of anguish,
I called out to you.
In the throes of despair,
I pleaded with you.
In this machine of suffering,
I prayed to you.
But in the bondage of thoughts,
I heard no answer.
So I dwelled in anguish,
In despair and suffering,
Until at last I found you —
Ever present, always with me.
Oh Lord of Everlasting Peace,
No praise is too great
For your glory!

Confusion about God

Wow ... where to begin here? There is so much confusion about God. I suspect even the gods are confused about God. So we have our work cut out for us here. With so many gods, concepts of God and gods, images of gods, and so many religions, sects, teachings, and philosophies, how are we to make any sense of the divine?

Of course, one answer — and not a bad one I may add — is to pick a respected tradition and just go with it. True understanding does not come at the beginning of a journey, but at the end. One does not set out upon an unknown path already knowing what lies ahead. One must tread the path sincerely to find out.

This is my main critique of those who dismiss or critique religious paths. Generally they consider the beginners' orientation — the simplest, the most dumbed-down and abridged, word-bound version of a religion — and draw their conclusion immediately. "Yeah, that just doesn't do it for me. Doesn't make any sense. I can't believe that."

No wonder there is confusion! Of course it doesn't make sense if you don't really know anything about it. And the kind of knowledge I am talking about only comes from direct experience — hard won through actually walking on a path — not through thinking, Wikipedia articles, or Comparative Religion courses.

That being said, this is not the only way. Actual lives are complex, and each one has its own path. The various traditions themselves are not really binary propositions. They are just so many pointing fingers, more suggesting a direction for seekers than determining one. The actual path one takes is unfathomable.

However mysterious our path is — whether it follows a particular tradition or not — and however much confusion we have regarding the divine, if we have just the smallest amount of faith in the direction so many fingers are pointing, we will have some idea where our path is meant to go.

GOD AND GODS

Because it's part of our cultural history, many people in the West have grown up with the story of how monotheism replaced polytheism. When I was little I certainly learned this story in a number of ways. We usually interpret the story as a sign of intellectual and spiritual progress for the community, with the monotheistic view being regarded as a more sophisticated and accurate representation of the divine. What we generally fail to recognize or appreciate is that it is still a *representation* of the divine. And because we have banished all other gods, we have no reminders that our god-image is just one image among many. And so we have ended up with a handful of monotheistic traditions all fighting over whose image is the right one.

This doesn't seem like progress, so much as the old tribal god-image conflicts playing out on a larger canvas. The same ignorance is present, and we end up turning the particular traditions themselves into idols, which we fervently worship or desperately despise.

As usual, it is ignorance itself that we are most ignorant of. We do not see our own idolatry, but rather project it onto others. Nevertheless, whether our god-image — idea, concept, story, tradition, et cetera — exists within a pantheon or a sort of monotheon of the mind, it is *still* only an image.

So much confusion about God comes from mistaking a representation of God for divinity itself. This is what some of the traditions themselves call idolatry. Of course, they warn against it, but ironically, I think this mistake is made a lot in monotheistic traditions. Because they project idolatry onto others, because their own representation is abstract and singular, it is less obvious that it's still only a representation.

In short, whether we view our god as one among many or as the one true God is not as important as whether we treat this view as the divinity itself or as pointing *toward* a divinity which transcends views altogether. Throughout history, in every age and every tradition, many have fallen into idolatry … but a few — by the grace of God — have realized the transcendence of God's being.

DIVINE ORDERS AND HIERARCHIES

When we do not treat the divine as transcendent being itself — beyond words and concepts — we tend to treat it as a particular being or beings. When we imagine an ultimate truth, love, or power and start giving it qualities and attributes we can relate to, we are already treating God as a particular being or a multitude of beings.

Many traditions — even so-called monotheistic traditions — divide these beings into various orders and hierarchies. And so while there may be a high God, there might also be lesser gods and demi-gods or there might be angels, orders of angels, spirits, demons, and so on.

A survey of cultures, present and past, reveals a staggering array of beings. Their qualities and attributes are as diverse as the universe itself. They are blissful and benevolent, wrathful and malevolent, mischievous and alluring, comforting and terrifying. They inhabit the natural world, other worlds, and cosmic dimensions. They manifest in dreams, in visions, in physical form, and in other beings.

How can we make sense of such divine diversity?

The mind itself delights in imagining and reimagining such things endlessly. So our tendency is to accept or reject whatever particular stories we hear about divine beings. This allows us to imagine or reimagine according to our current inclinations, thoughts, and ideas.

When in search of the truth, however, just accepting or just rejecting are both mistakes.

Spirits and ghosts, asuras and devas, angels and demons, wrathful and benevolent deities — such beings can actually be encountered. But when we accept or reject any aspect, story, or belief about such encounters, we turn them into a fixed view. In doing so, we may bolster our current view or adopt a new view. Either way, we are ignoring actual experience in favor of a view.

If we are to have any hope of really making sense of divine beings, we might take our actual experience — whatever it is — as a starting point for inquiry. After all, as individuals, we too are part of the divine order of beings.

Every experience, be it of an angel, a demon, or a cup of tea, points to our own being above all else. In this way, all beings serve God. If you encounter an angel, by all means, pay attention to what it shows you. If you encounter a demon, by any means, do not give in to fear. But ultimately, my advice is this: understand your own being first, then see if any questions remain about divine beings.

God and Guru

In some Hindu traditions, devotees may venerate or even worship a guru as divine. We should address this because, certainly in Western cultures, there's a lot of misunderstanding surrounding these practices. And that's probably true even in the cultures where such practices originate.

When equality is venerated and individuality is worshiped, or when a high God is considered far above all, many people may view the idea of prostrating oneself before another human being as repugnant, ignorant, misguided, or foolish. Of course, they hold these views while ignoring their own repugnant deeds, their own ignorance, and their own misguided and foolish behavior.

Such are the follies of views and human behavior.

Ironically, while often criticizing such practices, the West has been shaped by what could be regarded as the greatest guru-worshipping sect of all time. That guru — Jesus — was called Christ and is, of course, venerated and worshipped as God.

To understand such practices in other traditions — or even benefit from them — it's important to understand a little about the context in which they arise. Although Hindu traditions are incredibly diverse, many see God as permeating everything, and that the ultimate reality — Brahman — is both God and true Self.

With this understanding, God, guru, Self, other, and world are not separate, but one and the same reality. The guru appears in the form of a person who teaches or passes on this understanding.

A devotee or curious onlooker may mistake the guru for that person's mind or body, but for the true guru, there is nothing but reality itself.

If realized, the guru does not put themself above others. In fact, such a guru makes no distinctions at all. That guru sees and experiences all that is as God, as one Self, and as Brahman. To that guru, all are the same. If inclined to speak, the guru says "You too are that," while accepting any devotion as expressions of love itself. "Realize what you are," the guru says. "See that you are in God and God is in you, and you will know there is nothing but that which is called God, the Self, and Brahman."

As a devotee who still makes distinctions, it is not necessarily wrong to regard the guru as divine. For divinity permeates all of reality. Such veneration is simply deep respect and love for that one who has realized the truth and brought it to our attention.

GODS AND BUDDHAS

There are Buddhists who will tell you that Buddha is not a god, that Buddhists don't believe in God, and that there are no gods in Buddhism. Okay, fair enough. But such declarations involve interpreting Buddhism a particular way and interpreting God a particular way. And if there is one point I would like to make here, it's that God is not particular. Neither is Buddhism for that matter. And neither are you.

There are certainly many Buddhists who regard the Buddha in a way that seems strikingly similar to deity worship — even if it is in the form of a kind of guru worship — and many who venerate various buddhas and bodhisattvas as something strikingly similar to divine beings. Many teachings in Buddhism also describe ultimate realities that seem to point toward something very much like what we might call God.

Of course, we could say all those Buddhists are just doing Buddhism wrong, but we would be dismissing vast swathes of Buddhists and distinguished Buddhist traditions. So it might be better to say Buddhism points to something like God, but it is not our concept of God.

Such misunderstandings always come down to our idea of God or our conception of the divine. What we are really saying when we say there is no God in Buddhism is that there is not the kind of God that we imagine — the kind of God we have been conditioned to think of as God and believe in or not believe in.

But that kind of God is just in our imagination, anyway. We must admit that any real God would be beyond our ability to imagine or comprehend with a limited mind. Our imagination exists within or beneath God, not the other way around. Any other formulation would make God simply an object, and that is idolatry — something even the God-focused religions say is a mistake.

Within Buddhist teachings and literature, we find all kinds of ideas and concepts meant to distinguish the unreal from the real, and to point beyond. We encounter concepts like *sunyata* (emptiness), *tathata* (suchness), *dharmakaya* (truth body or reality body). And of course there is also *buddha* and *nirvana*. Even these — and they are just ideas — shift and change from text to text, era to era, tradition to tradition. But in some way, if taken as a whole, we can see they are all pointing to something ultimate, something beyond the imagination of individual ego-minds, something that is beyond all things.

Remember that all these words, ideas, and concepts arise in cultural, historical, and psychological context. Perhaps the Buddhist approach to ultimate truth, ultimate power, and ultimate reality avoids god-like terminology in order to avoid the confusion, mistakes, and spiritual traps such ideas sometimes come with. They are picking their battles, no doubt, but they aim for and are still pointing toward the limitless One.

If you ask me, "Is God real?" I will tell you, "Of course God is real. The questions is: what are we talking about? Find that out and you will have no more doubts about God." In the end, we must realize that God is beyond all imagination, beyond all ideas, beyond all concepts, beyond all words. That God is not absent from Buddhism … or even from atheism. In fact, one might argue that the realization of this God is the whole point of Buddhism.

RELATIONSHIPS WITH GOD

Regarding humanity's relationship with God, the spiritual literature and conceptual traditions are so diverse — inducing so much confusion if taken as whole — that we may be better off sweeping it all aside and just seeking answers directly. But let's first throw ourselves into the confusion once more. If for no other reason, it may at last reveal our ideas as nothing more than a tangle of thoughts mistakenly put before an ever-present reality.

In Jewish, Christian, Islamic and other Western traditions, we find ideas like God's children, the prophets, the messiah, saints, sinners, heretics, and infidels, as well as the saved, the unsaved, and the damned. These ideas have been defined and redefined and debated through the centuries. In the end, seen dispassionately, it's clear that ideas, concepts, and metaphors determine the course of human traditions and their relationships with each other much more than their relationship with God.

In Hinduism, Buddhism, and other Eastern traditions, the story is largely the same, but with some variation in the ideas, concepts, and metaphors. Here we find ideas like devotees and yogis, hungry ghosts and asuras, jnanis and buddhas, bodhisattvas and arhats. Again, as ideas, such terms are defined, redefined, and debated endlessly. That alone should suggest that terminology, concepts, and ideas regarding divine relationships are malleable. Only the absolute is absolute.

To some extent, terminology can be a helpful guide. Conceptual teachings serve as pointers along the path of one's life journey. According to culture and tradition, a particular set of ideas may serve to put one on the path. But it's all too easy to become enthralled with ideas and lose sight of one's quest for God alone. And as a result of so many ideas, many people treat their spiritual lives as little more than a battle of words, names, concepts, and affiliations. They imagine the truth resides in finding the right ideas, and in becoming the right thing, or establishing the right relationship.

Nothing could be further from the truth itself, which is always present, even in the midst of great delusion. Of course, the conceptual traditions map this idea as well, inventing levels of progression, attainment, and an ever-deepening relationship with the divine being. Until at last we come to the idea of going beyond all ideas, of going beyond relationship and realizing oneness, unity — the eternal and indivisible being, which is the true nature of all that is.

TRANSCENDENT CONCEPTS

At the end of any long line of conceptual teachings and various ideas about the self, the world, and what is happening lies the realm of transcendent concepts. Such concepts are still concepts, but they incorporate into them a kind of paradox, a mystery or exit point that directs our attention beyond. In other words, they are concepts that are deliberately not bound to particular meanings.

Such concepts ultimately point toward the infinite, the unbound, the indivisible, the all encompassing. They do so in various ways, of course, with a variety of images and ideas, but in the end what can really be said about that which transcends all things? Nothing definitive, that's for sure. All definitive statements are designed to limit. All that can really be done is to suggest, to point, and just say "That."

In spiritual discourse, across many traditions, there are so many transcendent concepts, and even limited concepts tend to lead to the transcendent ones. The great spirit, brahman, dharmakaya, tao, tathata, and of course, God, are all concepts which point to the transcendence of all things, all thoughts, all ideas, and all concepts. Words like samadhi, nirvana, Self, mind, truth, and consciousness also ultimately point to transcendence.

It would be tiresome to try listing all the transcendent concepts that have arisen from the world's spiritual traditions. In fact, to the extent that any particular tradition concerns itself with real transcendence, all its terminology begins to point in that direction, whatever the conceptual content. Something like "meditation," for example, may begin as a particular idea, activity, or practice, but it ends up encompassing all of being and non-being.

As concepts, all these ideas have definitions according to traditions that have changed and evolved over time. Taken as ideas, they have their uses, but if followed — if inquired into honestly — each transcendent concept must, in a sense, deconstruct itself. It must, in the end, point to a transcendence that is beyond even itself. For the transcendent reality is beyond words, thoughts, and concepts — even transcendent concepts. It is *beyond* beyond, so to speak. And the transcendent concept attempts to point overtly at that.

Whatever name we give to what lies beyond transcendence, all transcendent concepts point toward that, the all encompassing absolute reality. So when encountering such concepts, don't get lost in the weeds. Don't get caught up in definitions and distinctions, in beliefs and confabulation. Instead, look beyond to where the finger is pointing.

God and Reality

The usual way of thinking is to see the world and reality as the same thing. This is a mistake upon which so much confusion is built. Fundamentally, it is the same as mistaking a finger for the moon. The world points to reality, but is not reality itself. The world and everything in it comes and goes, appears and disappears. Reality, to be reality, cannot be other than absolute and eternal.

Only subjective, perceptual, intellectual, and imaginary realities have the luxury of flitting in and out, or being one way then another way, one thing then another thing. But in what do all these subjective worlds appear? From where do they come and go? What is reality itself? What is unchangeable and ever-present?

At the same time that we mistake the world for reality, we imagine God must be elsewhere, if anywhere at all. It is no wonder that even people of great faith struggle with doubts about God. By the usual way of thinking, God is not a part of what we think is reality. Even if we say the divine is present in the world, we fail to see it. And so we struggle to recognize the ever-present reality of God.

Furthermore, while we may think we know ourselves, in fact we see the self as separate from the world and reality — and also separate from God. So we doubt ourselves as well. We are adrift. We do not really know the world, or reality, or God, or even ourselves. And of course, suffering results from our ignorance and confusion.

How can we expect to know God if we do not even know ourselves? How can we expect to understand the world if we do not know what is real and what is unreal?

If we are ever to find the truth, everything must be examined carefully, without ignoring anything else. Otherwise we will always come to conclusions based on ignorance.

If the world as it appears seems real to you, start there. Examine carefully, through direct experience: What is the world? To whom does it appear? What is real and what is unreal?

Don't accept anything less than absolute and total truth!

If these questions are resolved with this condition, words will no longer confuse you. The nature of God and the nature of reality will become obvious.

We often assume we know what we're talking about when we use a word or recite a definition, but we really don't know what we're talking about. I can assure you. It's all relative — an ever-shifting landscape — until you realize that to which all words point.

THE LORD IS ONE

"Hear O' Israel, the Lord our God, the Lord is One." These words from Deuteronomy really get to the point. They are repeated by Jesus when some scribes ask him "What is the greatest commandment?" And they are echoed in Islam with *tawhid*, a central concept stressing the oneness of God. This total unity, absolute oneness, is at the heart of the God question.

Ordinarily, in the West, we might be tempted to interpret these statements as mere reflections of monotheism. But the oneness of God goes way beyond that. Instead, I would say the idea of monotheism is more the reflection here. We know this because the oneness of God is also found in polytheistic traditions and even in what some consider atheistic traditions.

In Hinduism, with its great diversity of gods and goddesses, the concept of oneness is central. Behind all apparent diversity, there is fundamental unity. That is the idea. In the Rig Veda, one of the oldest religious texts found anywhere in the world, and one of the essential texts of Hinduism, it is said that "The Truth is One, although Sages give it various names." And within subsequent Hindu philosophy is a rich and deep exploration of this notion of oneness.

In Buddhism, which many consider an atheistic tradition, concepts of oneness also hold a central role. Although they may give this oneness different names, conceptual names related to Buddhist ideas, all-encompassing oneness is still, by any other name, all-encompassing oneness.

From the scientific viewpoint, we may speak of the oneness of reality itself. Normal everyday science doesn't generally acknowledge the oneness of this reality, perhaps because there is not much science can say about absolute oneness. It is, in fact, beyond all scientific concepts and models. Nevertheless, deep thinkers in science will acknowledge that their models are only models, and that reality itself is beyond them.

When examined, unless you become confused by words and conceptual viewpoints, all avenues that point toward absolute unity and oneness begin to sound the same. God is one of the names by which we point to this oneness. But it is actually beyond words, concepts, and names. The oneness of God is a oneness that is so radical, so complete, that the ordinary mind — which holds itself separate — cannot comprehend it.

BE SILENT AND KNOW THAT I AM GOD

If the mind cannot comprehend oneness, how are we to realize God? This is a good question. In one form or another, it is the essential question of the spiritual endeavor. It's all well and good to say "Don't mistake a finger for the moon," but what good does it do us if we still don't know where to look?

When I was younger, I became very interested in spiritual enlightenment, but there just didn't seem to be any way to get there. I seemed to be missing something, and I couldn't comprehend what I was missing. Later in life, I tried to cultivate faith in a God that was beyond my comprehension, but the peace of the Lord was still absent. Anybody who sets out upon the spiritual path with honesty and determination will encounter this problem in one form or another.

At every step, we may think, *What is one to do?* But that is precisely the wrong question. Oneness is all encompassing! We cannot be apart from it. And so all our attempts to find it or reunite with it or attain it are sustained by ignorance — by a fiction of our own making.

Within this fiction, we may seek and seek, but that which we seek is ever-present, always here and now. Realizing oneness is not a matter of doing anything, finding anything, or acquiring anything. Instead, it is a matter of letting go of our ignorance, of dropping the fiction of our separation, and of surrendering the body and mind.

In other words, the path to the truth is not a path of addition, but of subtraction, of removing from view everything that is unreal and untrue. We do not acquire the peace of the Lord or knowledge of God, but rather we uncover it when all obscuring views are dropped.

Ordinarily we identify ourselves by discrimination. "I am so and so," we say, or "I am such and such." But these are only thoughts. If we trace such thoughts backward, dropping off bits and pieces as we go, we may experience some insight into the path.

First, if we drop the "so and so" and the "such and such," we are left with "I am." Recognize the essence of just being. Then, if we drop the "am," we are left with just the thought of "I." It does not have existence nor any other thought or distinction attached to it.

Now … what is before the "I" thought?

It may seem as if this is just a linguistic game, but I assure you it's not. We asked earlier: if the mind cannot comprehend oneness, how are we to realize God? The answer is simple. The mind itself is an illusion composed of thoughts. Only in stillness, in silence, can we know the everlasting Peace of the Lord.

6

THE METHOD QUESTION

I tried everything
I could think of …
Until at last,
I couldn't think
Of anything at all.

Confusion about the Spiritual Path

All honest seekers of the truth encounter confusion about the spiritual path. How is one to proceed? That is the most fundamental question. What can one to do? Which tradition holds the key to unlocking the mysteries of one's life and destiny? Which explanation is correct? Which teacher is the most enlightened? What are the levels of attainment? What method is most effective?

Following a spiritual path is often equated with choosing a particular religion, tradition, or method of practice, which become objects of identity. So we might say "I am a Christian," "I am a Buddhist," "I practice meditation," or "I'm spiritual but not religious." On the other hand, we may reject such things, and instead identify with atheism, agnosticism, science, or something else.

There are many views we may have about ourselves and the spiritual path. And while such views are sometimes helpful on the path, they can also be obstacles. And so it's important to note that they are just views; they are only thoughts. The actual path is much bigger, much more pathless, if you will. In fact, as I have suggested, it may be considered the entirety of your life, as it is.

Mistaking the thought-objects of a limited identity with the reality of our spiritual path is the source of a lot of confusion. At various points in our lives, we may follow one tradition or another, believe one thing or another, and do one practice or another. While all this may change, the path is the path, all along.

We may have many specific questions along the way. What is the goal? Is God real and what does that even mean? What is prayer and how should I pray? What is grace? In what posture should I meditate? How is sabija samadhi different from nirvikalpa samadhi? If we think we know the answers already, to some degree, we are already confused.

Investigation into the truth itself is where the path lies — not in words and definitions. The reality of our experience and the disposition of our hearts is our greatest guide.

AGE OLD VERSUS NEW AGE

People who are interested in spirituality are often confronted with a dizzying array of possible directions to explore. Where is one to look for guidance, for teachings, and for illumination? Not only are there all the traditional age-old religions and approaches, but there are also less traditional approaches, and then there are modern approaches, new-age ideas, and contemporary teachers not linked to or limited by a particular lineage or tradition.

How is one to make sense of it all?

On the one hand, we can be tempted to think that the established traditional religions must be onto something, as evidenced by their longevity. Surely they have figured some things out through successive generations of practitioners. And they can point to the saints, buddhas, or jnanis in their lineage to prove it. Of course, we can also be tempted to think that these traditions have surely become stale, lost the essence of the spark that may have started them, and become ill suited to modern people.

On the other hand, we can be tempted to think that there is a kind of evolution of spiritual ideas and that the new-age alternatives represent the latest insights. Surely a path that has come out of our own age is more understandable and more suited to guiding us toward the realization we seek. Of course, we can also be tempted to think that all these new-age ideas are a bunch of hokum, and that the people who espouse them are all deluded dreamers, con artists, and cult leaders.

Sadly, none of these thoughts are really well founded. If we were to always follow one or another of these ideas, we could easily be misled and prolong our suffering.

In every age — old and new — there have been enlightened beings who have realized their true nature and who live and teach accordingly. In every age, there are old traditions that have grown stale and old traditions that have preserved the essence of the original teachings. In every age, old ideas are adapted to the present, and there are new ideas, new practices, and new ways of teaching the truth. And in every age, there are tricksters, deluded dreamers, con artists, and cult leaders.

Nobody is spared this confusion. The spiritual landscape is a labyrinth of conflicting ideas and methods.

On my own journey, I explored meditation, Christian worship, service and prayer, Western and Eastern philosophies, Buddhism, Hinduism, yoga, martial arts, as well as a number practices that were, for me, more experimental, like self inducing out-of-body experiences, lucid dreaming, and detailed visualization. I did all this in a lifelong effort to find the truth of everything — of all existence and nonexistence. Although I didn't always know that's what I was doing.

There *is* an end to this journey, and it is far more wondrous and relieving than you ever would imagine. However, when we're in the midst of it, nothing is clear to us. We cannot even imagine the actual goal. We must strive on with little to guide us but our desires, our ideas, our dreams, our aspirations, and our suffering. It's no wonder the journey can be difficult at times.

Because we are conditioned to focus on particulars and easily become entranced by them, we tend to think the truth is something particular. So we spend a lot of time trying to figure out if it's this or that thing — this or that philosophical, religious, scientific, or metaphysical view. But the truth can be found everywhere and in anything — even a rock.

If you are rooted in an established tradition and engaged in practice, that's great. Go deeper. If you are dabbling in mysticism and new age philosophies, that's great. Go deeper. Wherever you are, find the most sincere, experienced, and selfless teachers. Pay attention to the commonalities between traditions and teachings.

The words may change, but the truth is always the same. It does not vary from age to age or culture to culture.

The truth is not a particular thing, and it cannot be grasped by the limited mind. But it *is* the truth alone which sets us free.

RELIGIOUS DEVOTION

The most common introduction to spiritual ideas and practices are the various religious traditions, most of which have some form of worship, prayer, and devotion. They are often presented as a path to the truth or a path of righteousness. But what is worship? What is prayer? What is devotion?

At the beginning of such a path, the answers may seem obvious. You go to the church, temple, mosque, or wherever and you do certain rituals, you say certain words, maybe you ask for help or guidance, and you do this regularly. But if you are serious about such a path, these answers rarely satisfy for long. And the questions must be looked into deeply.

Why am I doing this? What is the purpose of these rituals? Who is on the other end? Who is on this end? What exactly is going on? Where does all this lead, or do I just keep doing this stuff until I die so I can say I did my part? Is it just a matter of following the rules and doing the prescribed things?

Again, it's all fine to follow the rules and do the prescribed things. That's good. But if you are serious about this religion thing as a spiritual path, a method of approaching God, the truth, what have you, then there are no easy answers, and seeking them is a part of the path that is your particular *sadhana,* or spiritual practice.

At some point, we must loosen our grip on the particulars — the stories, the doctrines, the trappings — of our religion and ask: what is fundamental? What and where is this God I am supposedly worshiping? How do I attain this salvation or enlightenment the great teachers say is possible? What exactly is the method here? It would be a great help to have clarity on this. Many religious leaders are themselves lost and without insight, but there is a common methodology implied by the various traditions.

In the broadest sense, worship is the acknowledgement of a higher power, something greater than your ego-self. All such acknowledgement is worship. And all our various rituals are ways of marking, remembering, and deepening this acknowledgement. The fruit of worship is prayer. Prayer is trusting in this higher power. Whatever form our prayers take, it is trusting or attempting to trust in something greater than ourselves. The fruit of prayer is devotion. Devotion is love for the higher power. As love increases, the ego decreases. And finally, the fruit of devotion is profound surrender — a letting go of the individual self, a breaking down of all separation, a union with God.

That's one way of looking at it. But it's not enough to be told this is the path and where it leads. As you are probably well aware, it seems like a difficult journey. It is, however, the great purpose and destiny of life, so we cannot be satisfied with mere words. We must find out for ourselves the answers by walking the path, asking the questions, and relentlessly seeking the truth — which is a glory beyond any particular answer.

MORALITY AND BEHAVIOR

In the context of both religious and secular paths, morality — ethics, right action, good behavior, and so on — is touted as part of the spiritual path. Codes, rules, laws, and commandments that guide human behavior, whether spoken or unspoken, written or unwritten, are universal. This guidance on right and wrong, good and bad behavior, is on some level seen as a method for acting in accord with the spiritual path, or even as the path itself.

If you do these things which are good, you will progress spiritually and will get into heaven. If you do those things which are bad, you will not progress spiritually, will not get into heaven, or worse, you will be cast into hell. According to this model, some types of behavior bring you closer to the divine and some take you farther away.

If we look at the different rules, while they largely agree on some major points, the details can vary quite a bit from tradition to tradition, culture to culture, time to time. We might conclude, therefore, that any particular set of rules is not absolute, but rather is attempting to point.

God is omnipresent! Enlightenment is reality itself! One cannot come closer to the truth nor drift farther away. It's always there. The truth is the truth, even in the midst of great delusion. So whatever your actions, you are in it, but that doesn't negate cause and effect. Good is still good, and bad is still bad.

From the spiritual perspective, laws governing behavior are methods of guiding one out of delusion and suffering. Clarity and diminished suffering are what's good about "good." Delusion and increased suffering are what's bad about "bad." Ultimately, however, both good and bad are delusion. The truth is always present, and in the final account, all delusion is self correcting.

This is difficult to explain, because so many of us are clinging to very particular ideas about morality, about good and bad. We may be deep in delusion, but insofar as attempting to follow moral guidance challenges our view, disrupts our egocentric tendencies, curbs our selfish desires, then suffering is diminished and opportunities for clarity are created.

We have to have patience to follow such practices. They can take a long time to develop. It's not a matter of just being rigid and inflexible, nor is it really a matter of subservience to any authority or organization. It's a matter of orienting oneself to a loving kindness that diminishes suffering, and ultimately of understanding and unraveling the source of suffering itself.

SPIRITUAL BUT NOT RELIGIOUS

It's common these days to hear someone say that they are "spiritual but not religious." For one reason or another, such a person doesn't subscribe to any particular tradition. Perhaps they grew up in a religion but have rejected it on reasoned or emotional grounds. Perhaps they grew up without a religion and see no reason to join one now. Perhaps they are simply averse to any form of authority telling them what to believe and how to live. There are many possible reasons.

Whatever the case, a person like this still feels pulled toward the subject of spirituality. They may experience an intense longing that nothing seems to address, except the teachings and promises of the spiritual dimension. And while they may avoid traditional structures, they are still seeking the truth.

This is all well and good, but while we may avoid the structure of traditions for various reasons, we still face the same obstacles. And as is usually the case — religious or not — we may be convinced we have avoided the very obstacles we have placed in our path.

Religious persons, for example, may think they're avoiding idolatry by subscribing to a tradition that warns against it, as if by merely holding a membership card, they could avoid it. But that is idolatry already. It's not their fault, of course. It's all a part of the journey … and that's the point. Nobody escapes actually walking the path.

Spiritual-but-not-religious persons, on the other hand, may think they are avoiding the foibles inherent in subscribing to a tradition. But by avoiding one error and maybe patting themselves on the back for it, they ignore the multitude of other obstacles that lie in their way. In fact, when examined closely, one may find they are the same types of obstacles. Again, nobody escapes actually walking the path.

The advantage of an established tradition is that it provides us with a structure and a method for spiritual practice. But that very structure and practice rests on beliefs that can become distractions, rather than signposts pointing beyond. The advantage of being spiritual but not religious is that we can play fast and loose with our beliefs. But with little structure or methodology, we risk failing to do the hard work required for spiritual practice.

In my own search, I was for a time religious and for a time spiritual but not religious — and for a time not even that. I could say that I was lucky in getting through the various pitfalls, but the truth is that grace is always with us. As a practicing Catholic, I never thought I had found the truth or God — I was *seeking* God and would not be satisfied with less than complete revelation. As a secular skeptic or agnostic, meditation and martial arts kept me doing the hard work of what, I see now, was part of my spiritual practice all along.

We are all on the same path, whether we know it or not. And we all face the same types of obstacles. The advantages and disadvantages of various traditions, practices, and views is particular to individuals. But those seeking the truth, reality itself, or God, are seeking that which is beyond all particulars. The methods are multitudinous, but you have to do the work. Only you can discover who you really are and the truth that is beyond your existence and non-existence.

Big Compassion

In our endeavors to follow the spiritual path, it's important to uncover and cultivate our innate compassion. A wealth of traditions make clear that love and kindness are central to the path. Naturally, such practice often begins by focusing a spotlight on our own behavior, or by observing the causes and effects of suffering and joy, or by being more intentional about our everyday actions and choices. And that's all very good. But only by emptying ourselves completely can we discover a love and compassion that is all encompassing.

Teachings, practices, observations, and sometimes sheer practicality — even selfishness — demands that we cultivate loving kindness and compassion. It's a simple matter of decreasing suffering and increasing happiness. If a person can see and steadfastly try to follow this, they will be on the path, however many times they may go astray. But ultimately, the universe itself is guiding you toward a compassion that is bigger than any thought, choice, action, or individual.

We have all had the experience of being caught in the predicament of trying to figure out the right thing to do. Even when our intentions are good — to do no harm, to be kind, to not cause suffering — it's not always clear what course of action to take. And sometimes we tie ourselves in knots trying to work out in our little minds what exactly we should do, how exactly we should conduct ourselves.

At some point along the path it's good to aim for perfection. Try to see all beings as inseparable from yourself and extend loving kindness to them, without condition or reserve. Consider even those you view as the evilest and vilest beings and bring them within the loving arms of your kindness and compassion.

We have to try, even if our attempts may seem to fail or lead to confusion. But we have to have compassion for ourselves too, and ultimately, the only perfection possible is the one that is already present. Compassion itself — big compassion — is always at work and never lacking. Compassion itself encompasses everything.

So while we may make an effort as individuals or see our egos as lacking, those very efforts and perceptions are compassion itself at work. In this sense, real compassion is never ours, can never be commanded or possessed by the ego. But all love and all compassion — however small, however seemingly ego driven — is always pointing beyond, to a boundless compassion that is indistinguishable from reality itself.

Such a compassion does not live within us. Rather, we live within it.

MEDITATION AND CONTEMPLATION

In the West, the words *meditation* and *contemplation* can have a wide range of meanings, contributing to a lot of confusion surrounding spiritual practice. Some Christians even fear meditation, believing it will open themselves up to demonic influence. This may be more a fear of other religions and Eastern traditions than anything else, but fair enough, nobody wants to be attacked by demons — at least not without some instruction about how to handle such encounters. Nevertheless, there is a long tradition of Christian meditation, and a clear-eyed view could go a long way toward a better understanding of these practices for Christians and non-Christians alike.

Those determined to make distinctions will of find them — between meditation and contemplation, between Christian meditation and Buddhist meditation, or between one specific type of practice and another. But we should not confuse the forms of practice with the purpose or the ultimate goal. And therein we find remarkable similarity. Although the details of particular methods differ, and conceptual language surrounding practices and goals vary, almost all meditation practices really point toward wisdom and truth realization — beyond words and concepts.

In the Christian tradition, the word "meditation" can refer to a more cognitive practice of reflecting on doctrine and teachings. And so some Christians contrast this with Buddhist and Hindu meditation practices that emphasize quieting the mind, and even warn against them. Of course, they ignore Buddhist and Hindu practices of inquiry and reflection which are better suited for comparison. They also ignore the rich Christian practices of contemplation, contemplative prayer, and silent prayer, which include a variety of meditative practices aimed toward quieting the self, awareness of the divine, and ultimately, "perfection" or union with God. Such practices are really better suited for a comparison with Eastern forms of meditation.

Proponents of Christian traditions — even the Pope — warn against self absorption and the mere pursuit of ecstasy, which they usually equate with *other* meditative practices. Of course, they don't deny that practicing meditation or contemplation can result in ecstasy — there are famous examples — but they ignore the fact that other traditions have the same warnings against self (ego) absorption and the mere pursuit of ecstasy. In the Buddhist and Hindu traditions, for example, we can certainly find these same warnings.

So what we have, as is so often the case, is a confusion based in words. What is called meditation in one tradition is called contemplation in another tradition. What is rejected in the words of exoteric teachings is embraced in the practice of esoteric teachings. What is rejected in form is embraced in essence. What one calls the Holy Spirit, another calls prajna. What one calls samadhi, another calls silent prayer. What one calls perfection, another calls fana.

I don't mean to pick on the Christians here. The fact is that all the traditions make these sorts of mistakes, not only about other traditions, but even about their own traditions. The followers of various religions often don't sufficiently understand their own traditions. They have received some teachings and practices, but not knowledge — not wisdom. The struggle to understand and find wisdom is at the heart of all the traditions. Those who think they have things figured out are surely lost in delusion.

So whatever story we tell about our practices, keep in mind that the practices themselves are only pointing. We don't really know yet where they are leading us. That is why, however we go about it — meditation, contemplation, prayer — we better just get to it. Because the further one goes, the more meaningless words become, and all the distinctions we heretofore clung to begin to fall away. Whatever your tradition or practice, direct recognition of the truth is the source of all real wisdom.

TYPES OF MEDITATION PRACTICE

Today's popularity of mindfulness and meditation is a tribute to many beneficial effects. Meditation can lower stress, calm a turbulent or worrisome mind, and help establish baseline states that are more relaxed and rooted in a feeling of wellbeing and ease. In today's hyperkinetic, info-laden culture, such relief is desperately needed. So any step toward a meditation practice or calming the incessant mental chatter is generally a good one, worthy of praise.

However, serious practitioners of meditation may critique this trend in a number of ways. First, many modern practices are limited to achieving a superficial calming of the mind or attaining a few beneficial effects. Second, rarely is there any emphasis on inquiry and truth seeking. And finally, some of the real difficulties, challenges, and even potential dangers of meditation are rarely addressed.

A helpful distinction can be made between calming meditation and insight meditation, also known as *samatha* and *vipassana*. Many practices concern themselves solely with calming the mind through focusing. This is good, of course, but traditionally it's only a preliminary step. The ability to focus and the resulting calm are prerequisites for conducting the kind of careful observation and inquiry that is at the heart of insight meditation.

Likewise, there are some types of meditation that concern themselves largely with manipulating the mind to achieve desired internal states or to have particular experiences. Again, this can be good, but traditionally the goals of meditation go beyond … to emptying out the self and letting go of all particular states and experiences.

Whatever practice you undertake — practice itself being the most important step — move toward a holistic view of meditation. It is not one particular thing … and ultimately it is everything! And so all meditation practices have within them aspects of focusing, observing, manipulating, and emptying. Some may emphasize one aspect or another, but if one is attentive and determined, the whole is contained within the parts. So within your regular practice, cultivate an attitude of inquiry and a willingness to go where it takes you.

While there's nothing wrong with justifying meditation with a scientific explanations of how it may affect the brain and body, those relying solely on such explanations may leave themselves short changed. Meditation has been practiced for thousands of years, and traditional teachings on the subject contain deep wisdom. It makes sense to heed the advice of those who have learned from direct experience, even if their conceptual framework seems different from our own. When the goal is to go beyond concepts, such differences are ultimately superficial, anyway.

Relying solely on a scientific approach and leaving no room for mystery or traditional teachings could leave you high and dry if you, say, encounter a demon or enter a hell realm. Such experiences are possible — whatever you make of them — and they can be frightening, traumatic, and even devastating to one's well being, if left without proper guidance. Traditional teachings can provide that guidance based on the experiences of many generations of dedicated meditators. After all, I assure you, you are not the first person to enter a hell realm or experience other less-dramatic difficulties on the path. It is all a part of unraveling the mystery that is your self.

So, what are we to conclude? On the one hand, there are many types of meditation, with myriad names and conceptual underpinnings. We can do no better than to pick one that seems suitable and start practicing. Because on the other hand, there is just meditation, and ultimately there is not even that.

Samadhi and Higher States
of Consciousness

When we take up meditation or any serious training of the mind and body, we begin to explore the immense variety and possibilities of discovering and manipulating states of consciousness. Teachings on different types, levels, and depths of various states are found throughout the spiritual literature. As seekers it can be daunting and confusing to try to make sense of these teachings and to guide our practice accordingly.

It would be foolish to attempt to explain here the numerous possible states as defined by various traditions. What is meant by *samadhi* in one tradition is debated or refuted in another. What good can come of it? Concentration is concentration. Meditation is meditation. Samadhi is samadhi. Explanations point in various ways, and guide students along the way, but none of these states can be understood without direct experience.

Some traditions, such as Patanjali's eight-fold path of yoga, make numerous distinctions between types of samadhi with "seed," or meditation object, and without seed. Other traditions make fewer formal distinctions. With complex systems, there is the risk that intellectual grasping will waylay actual practice and experience. With simple systems, there is the risk of missing out on precise instruction. In either case, a good teacher can be helpful in guiding students from where they are in the moment.

Samadhi is a great example, but the spiritual literature is filled with names given to various states of consciousness: absorption, withdrawal of senses, expanded consciousness, stream entering, astral projection, lucid dreaming, ecstasy, kensho, satori, and so on. But can any progress be made simply through grasping at definitions and explanations?

If we approach our spiritual lives as merely an intellectual endeavor or as a collection of definitions that we accept or reject, we have stepped off the path. Or perhaps we've just stopped for a snack or to check for directions. Nevertheless, once we are somewhat oriented, we need to get back to the real work of sincere practice.

When speaking of meditation and states of consciousness, we must inquire into and explore these states through direct experience. There is no other way to really learn about them. So-called higher states of consciousness provide great opportunities for insight because of the enormous contrast they provide with our ordinary experience. I cannot stress enough, however, that while these higher states are indeed possible, attaining any particular state is not the ultimate goal of spiritual practice, unless it is to attain the state *beyond* all states.

So our practice need not be limited to so-called extraordinary states. When it gets right down to it, do we really understand our so-called ordinary states of consciousness? If we have not attained some level of samadhi, this should not discourage us. In truth, even our ordinary states of consciousness are extraordinary! For all states, from the most mundane to the most unusual, point toward consciousness itself. And until that is recognized, all states, however exalted, will come and go as fleeting experiences.

On Methods and No Method

Throughout this book, we have been pointing toward awakening, toward truth realization, toward enlightenment. We have been pointing toward the true self, toward non-dual awareness. Through many words we have been pointing toward the limitless One. But the question remains, how do we get there?

There are many prescribed methods, represented by the world's religions and wisdom traditions. Following such a tradition is certainly a start, and not bad one either. Such traditions have a wealth of accumulated experience and teachings from which to draw on. And this ordinary knowledge can be extremely helpful in orienting seekers on the path and sometimes in pointing them onward too.

However, no tradition has a monopoly on truth, and while some may be good at cultivating certain qualities in their practitioners, none seems to produce saints and realized beings with any more consistency than others.

Once we get into a particular tradition, initial bearings can be taken, rough courses can be set, and practice can begin within the prescribed method. But beyond that, there is still essentially no method. And by that I mean, we still don't really know how to get there. We can join a God-worshipping religion, and do the prescribed rituals, but to *know* God and the ever-present peace of the Lord is another matter. We can join a school of meditation, sit for hours on end, and even enter into various samadhis, but to enter into the samadhi that is eternal is another matter.

Whatever method we follow, whatever map we have of the terrain ahead, there is no substitute for actually going on the journey. There is no escape from actually doing the work and walking the path. There is no other way to really find out where it leads.

And while we're still on the topic of methods here, this seems like a good place to leave you with some practical advice.

The most important aspect of any methodology is not the particulars of its conceptual map or even of its practices. It is one's own effort — a sincere effort to penetrate its mysteries and find the source of everything. To maintain such effort, one's sights must be set on the highest goal imaginable, with an uncompromising will to the highest truth, an unassailable reality beyond words, thoughts, and concepts.

One of the most common pitfalls is mistaking progress for stagnation or failure. When we delve into a particular tradition or practice, we have particular results in mind. As we go deeper into the practice, we may have some extraordinary experiences, but they come and go, and the particular results we imagined have still not arrived — the peace or the knowledge that we sought after still eludes us. At this point, we feel our practice plateau or we begin to feel stuck. We might think the method is faulty or be tempted to abandon it and move on to another practice or tradition. But these plateaus that we experience and the resulting disappointments are actually real progress. Remember that the true teaching is disillusionment itself. Don't be surprised if you find it. Keep going! What's faulty is our own ideas, and we are being prompted — here and now — to transcend them.

7

THE ULTIMATE QUESTION

Within silence, all is heard.
Within emptiness, all is seen.
Within nothing, all is felt.
Both being and non-being fall away,
And within everything —
All at once —
The Great Perfection is revealed.

CONFUSION ABOUT ENLIGHTENMENT

It should go without saying, at this point, that there is a lot of confusion surrounding enlightenment itself. Why else would we be having this conversation? The words we use — enlightenment, realization, awakening, satori, salvation, moksha, gnosis, jnana, liberation, and so on — are all up for grabs. Is it real or unreal? Possible or impossible? Are they the same or different? Are there steps, stages, and levels? Is it a gradual process or a sudden happening? Is it attainable or achievable? Is there anything we can do about it? Does anything happen after it?

I admit I'm a little daunted by the prospect of sorting all this out in writing. And no doubt we won't sort it all out in a way that will fully satisfy to you, unless you have already realized the truth for yourself — in which case, you are already satisfied. By now it should be clear that our real purpose in addressing these topics is not to nail down particulars. Although at times that may help, our real purpose is to point beyond.

That being said, in the course of pointing beyond, I will try to make things as clear as I can. Particulars can also serve a purpose — to correct mistakes, to encourage practice, to clarify experiences, and so on. Ultimately, these particulars too are only so many fingers pointing beyond. So let's get into it.

Let's start by addressing a simple question that goes something like this: I had this experience or realized such and such idea ... is it enlightenment?

I would like to hear more, certainly, but if it is just a thought, idea, or experience, if it is something that comes and goes, I would have to say it is not enlightenment. At the least, if we are mincing words, it is not the fullness of truth-realization. It may be a glimpse or a significant insight, but it's not complete, unsurpassed enlightenment. It's important to be clear on this, so you don't waste time thinking you are enlightened already instead of continuing the important work of spiritual practice.

As I have said many times before, enlightenment is not knowledge or even understanding of a particular thought. Nor is it having a particular experience or being in a particular state. It is free from all thought. It is the reality that underlies and permeates all states.

The complete fullness of truth-realization leaves no room for doubt, and any thoughts that remain are quickly seen through, including the thought that one is enlightened. It will, I dare say, be fairly obvious that there is nothing beyond the absolute truth itself. You may look for something more, but it will be clear: this limitless One, this being-consciousness-bliss, this selfless Self is all there is.

The Two Awakenings

People tend to use words in a variety of ways, depending on their tradition and current understanding. That's perfectly normal, and consistent with everything we've said so far, but it can add to the confusion. Is awakening the same as enlightenment? Is satori the same has jnana? Is prajna the same as moksha?

No doubt there are subtle differences in the definitions, etymologies, and histories of the words. Those types of debates are only of marginal interest to us here. We are trying to cut to the heart of the matter. So it helps to understand, if it wasn't clear already, that what matters is not what word is used, but where it is pointing in any given usage.

Let's take "awakening" as an example, since it's a word that's used a lot in modern spiritual circles to point in a number of different directions. Sometimes it's used very precisely, at other times quite vaguely, and the direction is not always clear.

On the one hand, "awakening" is sometimes used in a way that is synonymous with entering into the highest wisdom. The Buddha, for example, described himself as "awake." And when we speak of his awakening, it is of that moment beneath the bodhi tree, when the morning star appeared, and through complete awakening, he became a buddha.

On the other hand, "awakening" is sometimes used to suggest becoming awake to the spiritual journey, progressing on that journey, or having a profound insight, an extraordinary experience, or a glimpse of the absolute. An awakening of this sort is more like having heard the teaching. When heard, the teaching takes root. It becomes lodged in one's heart, and a yearning and will for the greatest truth becomes a driving force in one's life.

These are both real possibilities for which a single word is being used. Of course that can cause some confusion. And even this feeds back into it. On the one hand, we might say that if there is any confusion or doubt about the matter, then one has not awakened. On the other hand, I have heard some say if there is confusion or uncertainty, then it is probably awakening. This is because people are speaking about two different kinds of awakening, pointing in two different directions. As with so many of the topics we've discussed, we see two version of the same word. We might say these two views represent a big, complete and sudden Awakening to the ultimate truth and a little, incomplete awakening, which is an ongoing process aimed toward the big one.

I don't really care how you use these words. They are only words. But … some who listen to the teaching do not hear, and some who have heard do not practice. Many do not believe complete awakening to the highest wisdom is really possible — they cannot imagine it — and so, of course, they always view these terms in the smaller, experiential, temporary sense. If they ever use them in the larger sense, it is usually relegated to more mythological cases. And in so doing, they may miss the larger point.

The greatest message I can offer is that real, direct, stable, and ongoing knowledge of the ultimate reality is possible. So I tend to favor speaking about the big Awakening and use words like insight, gnostic flash, glimpses of reality for the more extraordinary experiences that can happen along the way. Skillful use of words can definitely be helpful, and there are other terms and clarifications that may help us navigate this issue.

THE PANOPLY OF TERMS

In the Buddhist and Advaita Vedanta traditions, we are presented with the idea of two truths: relative and absolute, dualistic and nondual, samsara and nirvana. In the Judeo-Christian traditions we are presented with the idea of two realities: earth and heaven, worldly and divine. Whatever they are called, these two truths can be seen as relating to the two types of awakening already mentioned.

The small type of awakening relates to the arising of new, relative states from prior relative states, but in which dualistic views — subject and object, seer and seen, self and world — are, largely or in the end, still compelling. However exalted, such states are temporary and still leave one bound to the wheel of samsara. They may be more or less transparent, more or less clear, but they are still essentially worldly states that come and go.

The big type of Awakening is definitive realization of the absolute. It is not just a glimpse, experienced by a subject. It does not come and go. It is already present and eternal. It is not a state which arises and subsides. It is rather, that which underlies all states. It is reality itself. It is, therefore, entirely stable, even while transcending all thought and all experiences. It is nondual ... divine ... truly *beyond* beyond.

So if we examine the panoply of terms surrounding enlightenment, we find expressions of these two truths, of both relative progress on the one hand — intermediary steps, stages, and experiences — and of the absolute on the other. Some words, like *awakening,* can refer to both, depending on usage and circumstance. Others attempt to make distinctions between the two. It is usually a muddy mess that confounds any attempt to sort it out, particularly as it relates to the absolute, because words themselves are dualistic by nature.

For example, there are many different kinds of samadhi described in various Hindu and Buddhist traditions. They represent various states of consciousness and bliss. They describe and detail the temporary cessation of the senses, ego-self, and thought-objects, as well as temporary experiences of limitlessness, insight, and fundamental awareness. In some systems, specific types of samadhi are mapped out as levels of attainment along the path to enlightenment. That's all well and good, and can be excellent as a methodology for spiritual practice. But can there be different kinds or levels of the absolute?

The absolute, by its nature, is all-encompassing and without distinction. There can be no types, kinds, grades, or levels within it. To point toward the big enlightenment, what we need is a big samadhi — something like *sahaja nirvikalpa samadhi,* which is continuous and uninterrupted through waking, sleeping, and dreaming. Some speak of *mahasamadhi,* or great samadhi. I would suggest, perhaps, *eternal samadhi.* But then, these are only pointers. Nothing can really encompass the absolute, no matter how many samadhis we invent.

In Zen, they have the words *kensho* and *satori*. Kensho means "seeing essence" and is likened to seeing one's true nature. It is an experience one has, and so comes and goes as an experience. Satori is derived from the word meaning "to know" and so is related to terms like jnana and gnosis. Satori can be stable and transcends the distinction between the seer and the seen, the knower and the known. Although the words are sometimes used interchangeably, kensho can be seen as a taste of enlightenment, while satori is full enlightenment. Sometimes people speak of an "enlightenment experience," and I would say that is like kensho, because it comes and goes.

There are so many other terms that attempt to describe the big enlightenment: undifferentiated awareness, gnosis, perfection, union, consciousness without an object, sat-chit-ananda, moksha, liberation, prajna, bodhi, nirvana, et cetera. Usually these terms, like "enlightenment," are reserved for the big Awakening, except in cases where the speaker or writer cannot themselves comprehend limitlessness and do not believe it's possible to realize. So they end up downgrading terms in the context of their discourse, focusing instead on the attributes and sensations of various experiences and behaviors. But while the terms may vary, the absolute can never be something other than the absolute. And when truly known, there is nothing but that.

Exceptional Word Forms

When attempting to refer to the big enlightenment, teachers and writers employ a variety of means to suggest they're using words in an extraordinary way. Words usually refer to concepts, subjects, and objects. So when using them to refer to that which is beyond all things, special care must be taken to avoid confusion. Two primary strategies are common.

The first strategy is capitalization. We capitalize to suggest that the word is a unique, exceptional, and extraordinary usage of the word. So instead of "god," we use "God." It's not about turning God into a character named God. The capitalization suggests limitlessness. Similarly, instead of "self," we sometimes use "Self." Instead of "realization," we might use "Realization." Instead of "awareness," we might see "Awareness."

Capitalization is a way of drawing the reader's attention to the word. The reader might think, consciously or subconsciously, *Hmm, this is a special word, and it's being used in a special way. What is that about?* And just like that, the seeds of inquiry have been planted.

The second strategy is add-on words. Perhaps the most common add-on, at least in my own writing, is the word "itself." So "reality" becomes "reality itself," and "consciousness" becomes "consciousness itself." Instead of "awareness" we see "awareness itself," and instead of "enlightenment" we see "enlightenment itself." Another popular one is "as it is" or "as it really is," such as "seeing things as they really are." And so on.

How is "reality" different from "reality itself"? The "itself" draws the attention of the reader to the concept, in order to suggest or remind them that it is not what they think, that the actual referent is beyond concepts. In other words, there is a Reality beyond reality and that is reality itself. Don't let these words distract you from the real truth they are pointing toward.

In my work, I had some early readers suggest I should capitalize certain words like "enlightenment" and "realization" or I should go through and make sure I'm being consistent with such capitalizations. Fair enough. They were interested in making sure the text was consistent and clear, and I'm grateful for their advice. However, when I considered trying to be totally consistent in this way, I realized it was impossible. I would end up capitalizing everything — every word, every letter! And we all know how annoying that can be.

Exceptional word forms are more of a reminder than a distinction. Totally consistent application or over-usage would ultimately run counter to their purpose. The reader would eventually interpret these word forms as just another proper noun pointing to just another thing, maybe a special thing, but a thing nonetheless. When in reality, they are attempting to point beyond all things.

Post-Enlightenment Development

A lot of people want to know if awakening is a one-time deal or whether it continues, deepens, expands, or evolves. It's a fair question, but as with so many of these questions, if you make assumptions regarding what you're talking about, any answer could be misleading. It's best find out for oneself, but we'll go into it a little bit.

On the one hand, from the absolute perspective awakening is definitive and all-encompassing. It leaves no trace, erasing even itself. So the very nature of this limitless One means there is no possibility for future progress, for further improvements, or for deeper insight. There is no greater wisdom than Wisdom. And there is no greater truth than truth itself. We cannot get closer to it and we cannot drift away. Enlightenment is the full realization that our true nature is that. Anything that changes in this ever-changing world cannot change the limitless One, for it encompasses all things, all events, and all changes.

In this sense, awakening is true liberation and total submission, blessed salvation and utter annihilation. And yet, nothing has really changed aside from this Great Realization. For it has always been thus. Through all the confusion and suffering, through the ups and downs, sleeping and waking, births and deaths ... fundamental being — consciousness-bliss — has never wavered.

This complete enlightenment, this perfect wisdom, is not of the mind, nor of the body, nor of the phenomenal world. Mind, body, and world appear within it, not the other way around. It is not dependent upon conditions. Nevertheless, mind, body, and world may still appear. And while they do, understanding may deepen, loving-kindness may grow, teachings may ripen, and the reflection of this perfect wisdom may become clearer and clearer in every state that arises — be it waking, sleeping, or dreaming … be it in life or death.

The awakened person, however, has gone beyond the mind, body, and world, and is no longer compelled to identify with them. On the relative level, in this world, that mind and body are still subject to cause and effect. The body grows older. It may become healthier or sicker, and eventually it dies. The mind too may become sharper or duller. It too will eventually pass away. While present, these things change and develop as necessary and according to the situations in which they arise. The aforementioned deepening, expanding, evolving aspects of awakening are all a part of that mind-body evolution.

We see this reflected in traditional ideas and concepts, such as the two-truths doctrine, absolute and relative bodhicitta, salvation and deification, on earth and in heaven. One can see things both ways, but the absolute is always the absolute. So even after enlightenment, bodies and minds may still have work to do as servants of the Truth, but the enlightened one is no longer bound by body, mind, or world. Whatever arises, they are already liberated from it. Being at one with cause and effect, they are beyond all causation and all effects. They are at peace with whatever happens or doesn't happen.

Enlightenment and God

When people who grew up in Western traditions (Judaism, Christianity, Islam, et cetera) hear about the concept of "enlightenment," they tend to think it refers to something other than what their own traditions have been pointing to. Because enlightenment is associated with various Eastern traditions (Hinduism, Buddhism, et cetera) it's tempting to think that it does not point toward the God one has believed in or been told to believe in. But in God's light, there is no East or West, up or down, inside or outside.

The traditions themselves — their doctrines and dogmas, teachings and commandments, rituals and accoutrements — are not the truth itself. To mistake them as such is idolatry, a sin which leads to greater sins. The traditions are actually methodologies for spiritual practice. They are instructions on how to seek communion with the divine. Practice may involve many mysteries which people do not fully understand. Where are they pointing? Where else, but beyond.

God is the most high, the supreme, the eternal and absolute reality, in which all things have their being. If God is not That, then god is just an idea — just another thing — and is not supreme. Only the truth of God's supreme reality delivers us into the peace of the Lord's eternal presence. That salvation, by another name, *is* enlightenment.

I can already hear a thousand arguments from the faithful. But they all depend on specific doctrines, ideas, concepts, and intellectual objections. They all depend on presuming to know God without really knowing the Lord's eternal presence. But in that divine light, all are struck dumb. All ideas, all doctrines, all trappings of faith, indeed all distinctions whatsoever fall away in the bliss of divine Being.

Knowing God is not like knowing any kind of idea or thing or individual person. Perhaps this knowing is better likened to knowing nothing ... or knowing everything, but knowing it all at once, without any details or ideas, descriptions, words, or thoughts.

A billion fingers may point at the moon, but ultimately it is not a finger that you seek. So whatever tradition or religion you happen to follow or come from, do not assume you know the end from the beginning or the middle. Do not assume you know where it's all going, unless you have followed the path to the ultimate end. Then you will see that God is the beginning and the end, and encompasses everything in between, without limit or boundary. What tremendous, all-encompassing love!

ENLIGHTENMENT AND REALITY

I have said before that enlightenment is the recognition of fundamental Reality. I have pointed toward seeing things as they really are. And I have maintained that the enlightened state is nothing but reality itself. This is all well and good, and is certainly meant to point in the right direction, but if you think this Reality is just the everyday reality that you imagine, you would be missing the point.

Some people who hear such teachings take them as an indication that there is nothing beyond the reality of the world they imagine. Frustrated in their attempts to go beyond, they are happy to take "there is nothing to realize" as validation of their own delusions. This is a mistake. I can say so with confidence because it's a mistake that I made. Enticed by the idea of enlightenment but unable to find my way there, I took my life and the world as it appeared to me as reality. And I struggled with this throughout the remainder of my spiritual journey.

When I say "reality itself" or "Reality" or even "reality," it is not meant to point toward your body-bound ego-self and the material world it inhabits, nor any individual being or any world that you imagine. It is meant to point toward the source of all that — indeed, toward the source of all being and nonbeing. It is meant to point toward the groundless ground of all phenomena. It is meant to point toward the vastness of emptiness itself.

So when we hear that there is nothing to learn, nothing to teach, nothing to realize … while this may be so, don't get the wrong idea. This "nothing" is the source of all wisdom. It is quite profound. And it is more *real* than anything you imagine to be real.

And when we hear that we should be "realistic" about our life and expectations, about our spiritual aspirations, and about our practice … don't be led astray by assuming you know what that would mean. Do we know how to be "realistic" or what that would look like in the context of our life? Do we know what is real and what is not? Of course, be as practical as the situation requires, but don't assume you know what "realistic" is until you understand what is real.

If, through direct inquiry, we eliminate everything that is unreal — all impermanent phenomena — whatever remains is reality itself. The recognition of that which underlies all things — all thoughts, objects, subjects, selves, others, worlds, et cetera — *that* is enlightenment. Furthermore, the recognition and the reality are not separate, because you are not separate from it, and it is this underlying reality that recognizes itself.

ENLIGHTENMENT AND
CONSCIOUSNESS ITSELF

When seeking the most fundamental reality, it makes sense to look toward consciousness itself. Why? Because it is at the root of all our experiences, whatever they may be. It is at the root of all our conceptions, thoughts, emotions, imaginings, perceptions, observations, and so on.

But we have to be careful here as well. If we are not careful, you may again get the wrong idea. "Consciousness" is just a word, and people use it to refer to a wide range of different concepts and phenomena. The consciousness itself I am talking about is rather that which underlies all phenomena, including those which are commonly called consciousness, the mind, the waking world, and so on.

A body or a mind can be said to be unconscious or conscious in the common sense — asleep or awake, unaware or aware. In this same sense, we can be "conscious" of various things and events. These are various states which, like all objects, events, and phenomena, come and go. This type of consciousness is associated with subject-object duality. It always refers to *someone* being conscious of *something.* And the focus is always on these subjects and objects.

So what is beyond this ordinary consciousness? In other words, from where does such consciousness arise? If we go in this direction, these are the questions we should seek to answer. So, by looking toward consciousness, we are really looking for what is beyond ordinary consciousness — seeking the origin of all subjects and objects.

Don't get lost in assumptions. Many people will jump to the conclusion, based on what they have been told, that the brain is the sole source of consciousness. But where do brains appear? All brains appear in consciousness, as objects within it. Our own brains, in fact, rarely appear to us at all, and certainly do not appear, for example, in deep sleep.

What is the consciousness that remains, regardless of the coming and going of subject and objects, various perceptions, thoughts, and states? Before you had a body or before you stirred from deep sleep, what was your consciousness like? Was it not a consciousness without subject or objects — unblemished, pure, empty … limitless?

Some may call this *awareness* rather than consciousness itself, or the absolute, brahman, God, or the Self. But don't be confused by words. Enlightenment is the recognition of this original consciousness as ever-present and all-pervading. Whatever arises, arises within that … and really is nothing but that — a form appearing within the formless. So in sleeping, dreaming, and waking, it is always there — the groundless ground upon which we have our being and nonbeing.

Enlightenment is Real but Does Not Exist

Buddhism points the way toward enlightenment with the Four Noble Truths: the truths of suffering, the cause of suffering, the end of suffering, and the path that leads to the end of suffering. These are great! But for our purposes here, I would like to reorder them, and just focus on the truth about the end of suffering.

For most people, the truth of suffering comes without effort. Simply living our lives, we will come against this noble truth. As for the cause of suffering and the path that leads to the end of suffering, they are revealed by following the spiritual path. Rarely, however, will one set their intentions on this path unless they have imagined, intuited, or heard about the end of suffering.

For this reason, the greatest teaching is that enlightenment is possible. Liberation, moksha, nirvana, salvation, Self realization, union … all point to the reality of enlightenment. This is of vital importance, for it is the whole point of making the journey. It is what gives context to suffering. It is, in short, what makes the Noble Truths noble. In other words — words from another tradition — without resurrection and transfiguration, the crucifixion is just a tale of woe.

Enlightenment is real. This is the good news and my greatest, most heartfelt message to you. Unshakable peace, true happiness, limitless being, and bliss-consciousness are yours from the beginning. And it is possible to realize this, to enter into nirvana, and suffer no more. It is so real, in fact, that it is more real than anything you can think or imagine. It is more real than anything! It is, in fact, the only reality.

But the enlightenment that we talk about is still just an idea or a constellation of thoughts, ideas, and concepts. That enlightenment does not exist — or it only exists as an illusion for those still trapped in illusions. It is a helpful idea, of course — a most helpful idea, the greatest teaching even — that points to the reality beyond thoughts, ideas, and concepts. Once found, however, it is clear that this reality has always been with you.

Having never been absent from the light, how can one be enlightened or unenlightened? The real enlightenment transcends everything. It is beyond delusion and enlightenment. It is beyond even existence and non-existence.

A Billion Fingers
Point at the Moon

We started this discussion talking about words: their meanings, their histories, their ambiguities and difficulties. Before I started writing, I made a list of some words I wanted to touch upon. We covered a lot of them, but honestly, there were some we missed. Did we talk about shakti, kundalini, or the subtle body? Did we talk about dukkha? Did we talk about hesychasm or antar mouna? Did we talk about the trinity? I don't think so.

There are so many words, ideas, and concepts we skipped over, but that's okay. There is no way I could clear up all the confusion about words merely by addressing more words. Even if I had covered many, many more words, we would still be no closer or further away from the truth than we had been in the beginning. For as I said from the start: this is not a book about words. This is a book about the moon, and all these words — the ones addressed and the ones used to address them — have just been a way of pointing.

Hopefully this has become clear in addressing various words and concepts. Time after time, even while examining various definitions and ideas, we were simultaneously attempting to break down all conceptual differences. Even while throwing ourselves into the tangles, we were attempting to cut through them with the sword of truth. So by the end of every successful argument, there is no argument to be made. And by the end of every successful debate, there is no debate to be had.

We are so used to treating words, ideas, and concepts as truths, or at least potential truths, that even if we catch a glimpse of truth itself, we may disregard it. We may simply move on to other thoughts, ever looking for a more satisfying conjunction of words. Know — here and now — that no collection of ideas and concepts will ever satisfy the depths of your spirit. No definition, explanation, or cosmological view will ever reveal the truth itself. No finger can ever be the fullness of the moon.

Pick any one of the words we have addressed, go into it fully — look where it's *really* pointing — and you will find the truth. Or trace each word back to its source, and you will see that to which all words ultimately point. That is why all the various spiritual paths and religions are valid in their own right. They use different words, but follow anything to its ultimate end, and they all end in the same place.

So what's left after we untangle the language of spirituality? Nothing is left, really. That is why so few are willing to untangle it, and why so many are willing to merely argue over the definitions of words. *Words!* While all along, the nothing that is left if we go beyond them is reality itself, consciousness itself, and one's true Self, true God, and true Being.

We can always create and dissect meanings, stories, arguments, and explanations. There's nothing wrong with that, except the suffering brought about by mistaking such things for reality. But from the absolute view, all words are synonymous: god, self, reality, consciousness, matter … even tree, cat, banana, and so on. These are nouns, of course, but the same holds true for verbs, adjectives, pronouns, et cetera.

And it doesn't stop there. Everything is pointing! Every sensation, every thought, every dream, every emotion is pointing. Every forest and every desert, every mountain and every ocean is pointing. Every river that flows, every cloud that gathers, every rain that falls, and every sea that swells is pointing. A billion fingers are pointing! We have only to look — a shift in one's gaze is all that's required — and the fullness of the moon reveals itself.

APPENDIX

QUESTION AND ANSWER

As in each previous book, I have included a few answers to questions I've received. The answers are given in the abstract, and do not pertain to specific people. As always, I hope they will spark some illumination within.

Q: Isn't it presumptuous to say you are enlightened?

A: I am not saying I am anything special. In fact, it is you who insist on being something special, in that you view yourself as separate and distinct. I say that I am nothing really — nothing but reality itself. While you seem to think you are something more than reality. I take your point, and I understand how you see it that way, but there is nothing presumptuous about saying one has realized when one *has* realized. For that person, it is totally clear. I say it only because I would like you to know that true peace is possible.

Q: Are you saying there is nothing more you can learn?

A: Nothing can be gained or lost. The kind of learning you imagine — the accumulation of knowledge, the arrangement of thoughts and words, the categorizing of concepts and symbols — is not insight into the Truth. With insight, none of that other stuff really matters. Of course, practical knowledge has practical value, but ultimately, such things are only helpful when they lead to insight. Otherwise, they are the foot soldiers of ignorance. And always, they are impermanent.

Q: Do you still have desires?

A: The experience is different. What I would have before called desires arise, but they are transparent. This body still gets hungry, and tired, and so on. This mind still says "I want to eat" or "I want to go to bed." So in this sense, life is not so different. But I have realized fully that I am not this body and not this mind, so I am not subjected to these things in the same way. Desires affect the body and the mind, not the Self. I am not in the body or in the mind, or indeed even in this world. Instead, they are all in me.

Q: Is your behavior always perfect?

A: Although some people will misunderstand, I must say, as humbly as I can, yes. Everything that unfolds unfolds according to the way things unfold. If you take everything into account, there is no room for imperfection. There are never any real mistakes. Is it a mistake when the clouds form? Is it a mistake when the leaves fall? When the ocean heaves? When corpses rot? This body is no different. And neither is yours.

Realize oneness with all that is, and you will realize true perfection. Outside of this, there is no perfection.

Q: Isn't perfection more of a goal and a journey and not an immediate destination?

A: There is a popular saying that "The path is the goal." It's a good saying, but the way people understand it is not always right. Perfection is neither a goal nor a journey. Perfection *is* an immediate destination. That is the only way to realize perfection. The truth is always present and always perfect, but as long as we imagine it somewhere else or somewhere off in the future, we cannot realize it.

Q: A lot of respected spiritual teachers have been involved in scandalous behavior. Shouldn't an enlightened being always act with love and compassion?

A: I can't really account for the states of others, but compassion, loving kindness, and selflessness are all observable fruits of enlightenment. To be clear, enlightened being isn't anybody's mind or body — it is nothing but enlightenment itself, so there are no enlightened egos or individuals. An enlightened person could appear with some foibles or eccentricities, but truly bad behavior is always the result of deluded views and selfish desires. Practice compassion, of course, but don't ignore bad behavior. Bad behavior is bad behavior. Treat it accordingly. Just don't let the bad behavior of others dissuade you from a spiritual path.

Q: Do you think [a particular teacher's] teachings are accurate?

A: It's not a matter of accuracy. No teaching can be accurate in the way that you imagine. It's a matter of whether the teachings point people toward the truth and aid them in finding it or whether, if followed, they lead people deeper into delusion. That is the only consideration.

Q: How can I stop worrying about the future?

A: Rest assured that ultimately nothing can go wrong. Everything is happening now and this is how it's happening. If you are an action-oriented person, take what action is needed immediately. If you are an intellectually-oriented person, consider that you cannot do anything other than what you are doing and things cannot unfold any way other than the way that they are. If you have faith in God, know that God is always present, and the Lord's compassion knows no bounds. Remind yourself that all is well and under God's power. Above all else, always seek the ultimate truth, which alone can set you free.

Q: How should I pray?

A: First, by acknowledging God — by remembering that there is a higher power, whatever you want to call it. Then, by trusting in this higher power. Finally by loving this higher power. This could happen all in an instant, or it could be a practice that unfolds in time, even over a lifetime. Either way, these are the elements of prayer.

Q: What happens once you see through all your problems?

A: Nothing happens. But it's a lot more wonderful than it sounds.

Q: What does it mean to realize that a thought or feeling that is completely demoralizing is actually just a part of what's happening?

A: Things that arise have to be allowed to run their course without letting them trouble you. They have already arisen — what can you do about it? Thoughts and feelings come and go all the time. Every year winter comes and every year summer. You cannot stop it. You ask, "What does it mean?" There is separation and conflict even within this question, but you are on the right track — see it clearly and you will know what it means.

Q: What does the daily ritual and routine provide for a monk?

A: Ritual and routine helps one focus on practice, develop concentration, patience, resolve, and surrender. It's possible in any situation, of course, but effort is always needed.

Q: Why do religions focus on conventional morality if the truth transcends everything?

A: Although imperfect, it's a good starting place. One has to have some roots in conventional morality and compassion before seeking the absolute truth, because the journey can take us across some desolate and merciless lands. A person with no habitual compassion could become a monster before ever reaching an understanding of absolute compassion.

Q: It seems that even those who ardently seek the truth and listen to teachings, do not always find it. Is there anything you can say to make this journey easier or faster?

A: Everything I have said is to this end. The peace of the truth is always present and available. Look for that peace which is always there, and abide in that. During a Catholic mass, people turn to those around them and say, "Peace be with you." That is basically the way. May that everlasting peace be with you all.

ABOUT THE AUTHOR

On April 11th, 2016 Matthew Lowes had an unexpected and profound spiritual awakening, just as the great mystics have described. Since this enlightenment dawned, he has endeavored to communicate the insights intrinsic to realization and help others on their spiritual journey. In addition to this work, he continues to be a writer of fiction and games, as well as a student and teacher of martial arts, fitness, and health practices.

matthewlowes.com

Only you can find out who you really are.

LIGHTING
THE
SACRED
FIRE

MATTHEW LOWES

ENGAGING IN SPIRITUAL PRACTICE

An inspiration for spiritual practice that makes it clear:
Whatever tradition you follow and however you refine your view,
sincerity and effort are the most important elements.

—Coming in 2023

Thank you for reading!

Please post a review online. :)

The next book in this series,
Lighting the Sacred Fire,
is coming in 2023.

Printed in Great Britain
by Amazon